Relinquished

When *Love* Means
Letting
Go

Jamie ‒
Joel 2:25
Blessings ‒
Carrie O'Toole

Relinquished

When Love Means Letting Go

CARRIE O'TOOLE, M.A.

Published by Carrie O'Toole Ministries Publishing
Parker, Colorado
Copyright Page:

Cover Design: DJ Ramirez
Layout: Steve Plummer

Printed in the United States of America

Visit our website at: www.carrieotoole.com

ISBN: 978-0-9960228-0-4

"I can say from experience that raising adopted children is very challenging. It can be like having strangers in your house all the time. Those who have not experienced these things will have easy solutions. Easy Answers. This book goes much deeper, and will help couples considering adoption to know more of what they may be taking on, before they commit. Love does not conquer all; but through God's love and the support of mature Christian friends, we grow, especially during the most difficult of times."

LARRY O. SANDERS, M.D.,
BOARD CERTIFIED IN PSYCHIATRY AND NEUROLOGY

"Carrie O'Toole understands the value of relationships and attachment as well as anybody I know. Not only does she help others using these principles, she has a tremendous story of redemption that gives her the credibility to do so. My prayer is that each of us could experience the process of self-discovery and freedom that Carrie found. This book will help give you a taste of that process."

JOSHUA STRAUB, PH.D.
COAUTHOR OF GOD ATTACHMENT

"You'll be hard-pressed to find a more vulnerable account of a woman who's faced a dark night of the soul. Carrie has vulnerably authored an account of her tortuous journey to let us know that we are not alone in our struggle to find peace, both in ourselves and in our relationships. Speaking as one of her confidants through her difficult and lonely journey, I applaud Carrie's selflessness and strength. She shows us that we can trust in the sovereignty of a loving God. She is a true modern day hero."

MARY ELLEN MANN, LCSW,
AUTHOR OF BATTLE SCARS OF THE PRINCESS WARRIOR, PRESIDENT OF MANN COUNSELING GROUP, AND CO-FOUNDER OF LAST BATTLE

Dedication

To Sam: I wanted to be your "Forever Mommy," but it wasn't to be. I think about you and pray for you often. I hope you will grow up to be someone who helps feed hungry kids, and helps kids who can't sleep. I love you, Sam.

To Bob: Through it all, you are there. Thank you. I love you.

To Brendan: My first child! You've taught me how to love more deeply, to let go of my narrow-minded thinking, and to dream big dreams. I love working with you, creating with you, and spending time with you. I love you.

To Katie: My beautiful, talented, courageous, passionate daughter! I love when we get to go shopping and have lunch together. It only takes a few minutes, and BAM, we're off to the races talking. I love your heart, your music, your laughter, and your dedication to all things and people you love. I love you.

This book rose from the ashes of the darkest time of my life. It took God, and a whole lot of people, to pull me back from the depths. I'd like to thank them now.

Mary Ellen: I don't think I would have made it without your wise counsel, wisdom, humor, strength, and the courage you provided.

Larry: Thank you for not diagnosing me as "crazy." Thanks for the meds—they were so desperately needed for that season of my life. Thanks for calling me your friend after I was no longer your patient.

Kelly and Tom: Thank you for listening to God's voice and being willing to take on the exceptional challenge and blessing of parenting Sam. You said it wouldn't be pretty. You were right. Thanks for stepping into it with us. (Thanks also for the facial, when my eyes were sunken and my skin was pale).

Ed: Thanks for all the massages. You got the knots out, with tenderness toward my broken heart.

Dr. Boykin and Dr. Eric Shuemake: Thank you both for working on my spine, and helping me regain my physical health.

NewLife Ministries, Steve Arterburn, Milan and Kay Yerkovich, John Townsend, and Henry Cloud: Thank you for showing me what emotional and spiritual health looks like.

The women who knew me and didn't run away—Sandy, Monica, Mary, Garlan, Kelly, Marta, Ani, Lori, Joan: Thank you isn't enough.

All who encouraged me to tell this story.

Shannon Ethridge: Thank you for being my coach, mentor, and friend. Thank you for editing this book, helping me to "show and not tell," encouraging me to "put on my big girl panties," and guiding me to become the leader, author, speaker, and teacher I am today.

Words For The Journey: Thank you for the encouragement through "toots and claps!"

Sandy Utz: Thank you for being my best friend. For listening to my junk and sharing your own. Thank you for reminding me why it was important, over and over again.

Leah Campbell: Thank you for providing your heart to my voice as you edited my story. You understood where the pain was too great, and took over to fill in the blanks. Thank you so much.

Matt Rutt: Thanks for having such a great eye, and catching all the mistakes.

Foreword:

I'VE ASKED FORREST Lien, LCSW, Executive Director and Attachment Disorder Therapist and Trainer, to explain attachment, how children attach, what happens if this process is disrupted, and how to help families raising children with attachment disorders:

Many of us idealize the major events and celebrations in our lives. We often create blissful thoughts and images of marriages, births, and holidays. Often overlooked are the possible difficulties, frustrations, and disappointments. Adoption of a child is much the same. While many adoptions go well, many do not.

Many children up for adoption have been traumatized by their birth families, by foster families, by multiple moves in foster care, neglectful care in orphanages, and by physical, emotional, and/or sexual abuse. Too often adoptive parents are told, "All this child needs is love and everything will be fine." This is not always true. Whether using a state or private agency, adoptive parents need to be careful and have realistic expectations that you may not get your "fantasy child."

Many local television shows, newspapers, and newsletters promote the adoption of children by featuring two or three different children regularly. Two five-year-olds were recently highlighted with the following comments: "He's big for five but already knows what he wants." "He loves basketball and likes to play with toy cars and trucks." "He prays before he goes to sleep every night." "Her teachers say she's bright and well-behaved." "She enjoys singing and dancing."

Red flags that were never raised in regards to these children are, "He first came into foster care at the age of five months after he and three siblings were abandoned by their mother. He's been in five foster homes and one relative placement.... Although his brothers and sisters returned home, he did not because his mother was unwilling to accept his lack of attachment to her." Further, "His family must be able to work with his mood disorder and attachment problems." Another example: "She wants a lot of attention and needs to be in control most of the time...her therapist is helping her deal with past abuse and she is learning to accept direction and parenting from adults...she still sets herself up as the victim and blames others for things she has done."

Every parent, biological or adopted, should know as much as possible about the attachment process. Surprising as it may seem, few parents understand the importance and the life-long impact of this process on children.

Attachment is one of the fundamental biological processes necessary in most animals for survival of the species, along with reproduction, caregiving, caretaking, feeding, and environmental awareness. Attachment has been described as operating unnoticed, much like the physiological regulators that control our blood pressure and body temperature.

The attachment process begins in the first few months of a child's life. In developing the parent-child bond, the infant responds to the adult's (primarily, but not always, the mother figure) caregiving. Simply stated, it is a process that operates to enhance the safety and security of the infant and to aid the infant in getting his or her needs met through human interaction: touch, eye contact, smiles, motion, and food.

Currently many people still believe that babies and children can recover from just about anything and that not much affects or influences them. This fallacy has helped to create many harmful beliefs and behaviors toward babies and children. How well the infant is able to get its needs met in the first year of life has much to do with the child's development, not only physically but also psychologically.

This reciprocal process of a child bonding with an attentive parent influences whether the child develops recurrent feelings of anger or happiness, hopelessness or hopefulness, dissatisfaction or satisfaction, and distrust or trust toward his or her caregivers. The child begins to understand whether his or her world is a safe place or not. It has been estimated that by the end of the first year of life the child has learned 50% and by the end of the second year 75% of everything he or she will learn during life. Among the many things learned are how to have relationships with people, how he or she fits into the world, and methods of controlling external and internal influences over his or her life.

Children begin to develop attachment behaviors that are described as either secure or insecure. Insecure attachment behavior is further described as ambivalent, avoidant, anxious, or disoriented-disorganized, depending on a behavior pattern. The pattern of attachment behavior can be influenced greatly by what happens in the child's environment.

Children have the ability to attach on any level, even a traumatic one. While the behaviors must be thought of as operating on a continuum, it is clear that many insecurely attached children have behaviors that can be very destructive to themselves and others. These behaviors are not always apparent at first to the untrained eye.

As children, our brains organize relative to the environment in which we grow up—either safe and secure, or scary and sad. Our feelings are stored in the limbic system or midbrain. One of the most common adaptive behaviors in which humans engage is "pain avoidance." Thus, a child who's been exposed to a maladaptive (physically or emotionally painful) environment organizes his brain in a maladaptive style of survival behavior, also described as Post Traumatic Stress Disorder (PTSD).

This organization of the brain creates a tendency to function more from a cognitive place of denial (which is a function of the right frontal cortex) rather than integrating the limbic system (affect regulation) into appropriate cause and effect thinking. In other words, when the emotions residing in the limbic system are triggered, the frontal lobe jumps to attention with a strategy to defend or deny those feelings.

The two most common feelings triggered in these children tend to be fear and sadness. Once these feelings are triggered, their defenses go into action to protect them from those feelings.

CONTROL tends to be the primary adaptive behavior to keep them safe. These kids can utilize many types of controlling behaviors to keep the primary attachment figures away from them, especially a mother figure. Children with attachment difficulties want to be loved and accepted but don't have the "tools" to achieve that goal. Their cognitive/emotional distortions sabotage what they want and need most. The more intelligent the child, the better they are at manipulating their environment on their terms. Relinquishing control or being vulnerable to the control of a mother figure feels like they're going to die.

Adoptive parents are often set up for failure from the beginning because they don't have any awareness of the disorder. Mental health, social services, and adoption agencies typically do not have the clinical expertise to assess the severity of attachment problems, so parents go into the adoption blindly. Once the adoption is finalized, parents find themselves alone with the problem.

Excited about having a new child in the home, parents work hard to give the child love and support. Once the relationship becomes too close for the child, the symptoms of control will become more prominent. The harder moms work to solidify relationships, the more the children will escalate their behaviors to push the "nurturing enemy" away.

If there is a dad in the home, he may typically get charmed by the child because they exhibit different behavior toward the father. This dynamic can cause problems in the marriage. Outside the family, the child may exhibit superficially charming behaviors to extended family, friends, teachers, caseworkers, and therapists.

This makes the mom more isolated with the problem and feeling like a prisoner in her own home.

If you have a child with attachment disorder, you may feel:

- Isolated
- Depressed
- Frustrated
- Stressed

- Hyper-vigilant

- Agitated

- Frazzled

- Foggy

- Confused

- Obsessed with finding answers

- Blamed and misunderstood by everyone—therapists, social workers, friends, family

Attachment Disorder is the inability to form loving and lasting relationships, to give or receive love or affection, to form a conscience, or to trust others. Attachment difficulties are on a continuum of disturbances that range from attachment issues to attachment disorder.

Attachment disorder falls under many names and categories. In children, these names include: Reactive Attachment Disorder (or RAD), Oppositional Defiant Disorder, and Post-Traumatic Stress Disorder. The following is a list of symptoms that an attachment disordered child may exhibit.

SIGNS OF ATTACHMENT DIFFICULTIES (AGES 1–5)

- Excessively clingy and whiny

- Persistent, frequent tantrums, sometimes escalating apparently beyond the child's control

- High threshold of discomfort; seemingly oblivious to temperature discomfort; picks sores and scabs until bloody without manifesting pain

- Unable to occupy self in a positive way without involving others

- Resistant to being held

- Demands affection in a controlling way, on the child's terms

- Intolerant of separation from primary caretakers except on the child's terms
- Indiscriminate display of affection, sometimes to strangers
- Problems of speech development
- Problems of motor coordination; considered accident prone
- Hyperactivity evident
- Feeding problems
- By age five, may be manipulative, devious, destructive, hurtful to pets, frequently dishonest

SYMPTOMS OF ATTACHMENT DISORDER (AGES 5–14)

- Superficially engaging and "charming"; uses "cuteness" to get others to do what he or she wants
- Lack of eye contact on parental terms; difficulty making eye contact with others while talking with them
- Indiscriminate affection with strangers; goes up to strangers and becomes overly affectionate with them or asks to go home with them
- Not affectionate on parents' terms (not cuddly); refuses affection and pushes parents away unless child is in control of how and when it is received
- Destructive to self, others, and material things; accident prone; seems to enjoy hurting others and deliberately breaks or ruins things
- Cruel to animals; may included incessant teasing, physical assault, torture
- Steals from their home, parents, and siblings, and in ways that almost guarantees getting caught

- Lies about the obvious for no apparent reason, when it would have been just as easy to tell the truth

- No impulse control (frequently acts hyperactive); extremely defiant and angry; needs to be in control of events in his or her life; tends to boss others; responds with prolonged arguing when asked to do something

- Learning lags; often underachieves in school

- Lack of cause-and-effect thinking; surprised when others are upset by his or her actions

- Lack of conscience; unconcerned about hurting others or destroying things

- Hoarding or gorging food, or has other unusual eating habits

- Poor peer relationships; difficulty making friends or keeping friends more than a week; bossy in his or her play with others

- Persistent questions and chatter; asks repeated nonsensical questions or chatters non-stop

- Inappropriately demanding and clingy; tries to get attention by demanding things instead of asking for them; clingy or affectionate only when wanting something

- Development of abnormal or unusual speech patterns

- Sexual acting out; may act sexually provocative with peers or adults; masturbates in public

In closing, my heart goes out to all the families I've worked with over the past 36 years who have fought to find the answers for their broken child, and those that never did get the help they needed!

Forrest Lien, LCSW
Executive Director and Attachment Disorder Therapist and Trainer
Institute for Attachment and Child Development

Introduction

WHEN I BEGAN writing this book three years ago, I had no idea the journey that lay ahead. At first, the memories flowed so quickly, I could hardly type fast enough to keep up. I got it all out.

And then it sat in my computer. I talked to some publishers, but soon realized not many wanted to talk to unknown authors about their memoirs.

I changed the direction of the book several times. It became a self-help book describing the relationship styles I learned about through years of parenting my son, and through my studies at graduate school to become a Marriage and Family Therapist. The more I researched, the more I realized that other authors had already written what I was trying to write.

I started over several times, with several different approaches. My little book remained in my computer, but continued to tug at my heart. I needed to finish this book. I needed to have closure.

This book is the funeral we never got to have. It is closure to the dreams we'll never see come true. It is the death of the reality I longed for, which will never be.

Some names have been changed to protect the privacy of individuals moving forward.

Thank you for choosing to read this book. Thank you for honoring me with your time and energy. Thank you for caring. I hope that, in some way, you will relate to my story, because we all have occasions where the most loving thing to do is to let go.

Chapter One

DO YOU UNDERSTAND that relinquishment means you will no longer have any say in your son's life, that he and his new family may or may not choose to include you in his life, and that the decision you are making is a permanent one? Do you agree to sever your parental rights completely?" The judge looked solemnly at us both.

What had happened to our plans?

Bob and I swayed in a fog of dizziness as defendants on one side of the courtroom, while Kelly and Tom sat at the opposing table. The judge continued to interrogate us regarding the efforts we had made on our son's behalf throughout the years.

Yes, we had tried therapy. Numerous times with numerous professionals.

Yes, we loved him.

No, we didn't think his best interests would be served if he remained in our home.

Had the clock stopped along with my heart?

How could so few questions wring the life out of a soul?

My stomach shuffled its contents as my mind retraced the past decade.

How had it come to this? We had loved until it almost destroyed our family and took my life. We had pursued every type of professional help available. Counselors, therapists, educators, doctors, and church leaders had scrutinized our lives and offered what they could—all to no avail.

We were still here. Giving up. Like I had never believed we would.

I came back to my parents' words: "The world is not fair." My innocent young brain had misinterpreted this information. I had convinced myself that if I worked hard enough, I could reorder life's little inconsistencies and even things out. I was the type of kid who asked the teller at the bank for an extra sucker to take home to my sister when she couldn't join my mom and me on an outing. I shared my ice cream when my scoops seemed larger. I was always looking for ways to keep everything fair and equal.

Because life was not fair, I took it upon myself to make up for the irreconcilable differences I experienced.

This time though, I could not create wholeness, no matter how hard I tried. I felt our lives were a crumbling mess, and it seemed as though so many of the pieces were simply no longer there. Nothing I had done worked. Justice eluded me. How could I make sense of a world where this could happen to our family, even though we had done everything right?

"We understand, Your Honor."

Bob and I supported each other's sobbing bodies as we limped out of the courtroom. Even though we left minus one child, our hearts somehow took on more weight that day.

The judge granted our petition and showed extreme compassion. We would soon find out that others were not as kind.

Chapter Two

I GREW UP IN an upper middle class suburb of Denver as the second of four children. I led a fairly idyllic existence. Family time, camping trips, after-dinner bike rides, summer days at the pool, and Sundays at church filled my youth.

My sister, Shelley, was two years older than me. My brother, Matt, was four years younger than me, and our family adopted my youngest brother, Dave, from Vietnam when I was seven. He was 14 months old when he arrived. I fell in love with him immediately, and even took him to "Show-and-Tell" at school because I thought he was so cute.

Nothing ever seemed too difficult for me, and I believed I could accomplish anything, so long as I tried. For the most part, that theory proved to be true. My few failures included losing the student council election in 6th grade, not making the cheerleading squad in 8th grade, and ending up with only a small part in the chorus for the 11th grade musical. At the time, those deviations from my normal success seemed life altering and like the worst possible things that could happen to me.

Now, I know better.

I enjoyed softball and basketball in elementary school, had great childhood friends, and found a passion for music in high school—eventually becoming the drum major of the marching band. That excitement and love for music went on to shape the next 15 years of my life. My guidance counselor asked about my interests as I prepared for college. We discussed my love of music and an innate desire to help other people. She introduced me to music therapy, and with only a limited understanding of what the path entailed, I made the decision to attend Colorado State University, solely because it offered this degree program.

After only a single semester, I changed my major to music education. It turned out that Music Therapy hadn't been all I thought it would be. But it *had* led me to the university I now called home, and I remained at CSU for the duration of my education.

It was there that I met Bob.

He was 6'4" tall with dark hair, a quintessential '80s mustache, and long socks paired with O.P. shorts the first time I laid eyes on him. Remembering the look and how little it fazed me at the time still makes me smile today.

Bob also grew up in a suburb of Denver, the seventh of eight children in an Irish Catholic family. He attended 12 years of parochial school and used to regale me with tales of family trips to Montana, where his grandmothers lived. Their family station wagon held all 10 family members for the long adventure that typically included a stop at the A&W restaurant. Bob's dad always wanted to get to their destination quickly, so he chose the drive-in to order. He asked everyone what they wanted, listening tentatively as the varied responses came in. "I want a Papa Burger and fries," or "Get me a Mama Burger with onion rings." And then, he placed the same order every year: "Ten small burgers, and ten small cokes please!" This became a running family joke.

When it came time for college, Bob and two of his high school buddies decided it would be great to attend together, selecting a university based on the advice of a guidance counselor who helped them find a place that would meet all of their educational needs. And that was how Bob wound up at CSU pursuing a business degree.

He was a year ahead of me and was the dorm RA when I entered my freshman year. His job entailed checking IDs at mealtime, working the front desk, sorting mail, and planning activities for the students living on his floor. His sister started the year after I did, and happened to live just a few doors down from me in the same dorm.

Looking back, that first year of college was a bit tumultuous for me, primarily because of the relationships I chose to involve myself in. My naivety showed when it came to dating. I had grown up in a church family, and the people around us were mostly honest. My high school boyfriend had treated me very well, made me laugh, and never took advantage of me in any way. I entered college assuming that all future relationships would be the same, never realizing how poorly some people could treat each other.

My first college boyfriend, Derek, was in my band—a cliché in and of itself. He was the start of my education on men and recognizing the jerks from the good ones, and his eventual betrayal wounded me deeply. It was such a shock to my system to experience such disrespect at the hands of someone I had allowed myself to care about, that I went through a period of questioning myself and feeling less-than in the wake of our breakup.

Throughout it all, Bob was always just kind of there. And as my wounded heart pumped along, I began to notice him in my peripheral vision. Unlike so many of the other guys I had become acquainted with in college, he didn't spend his time hanging all over whichever girls would pay attention to him. He treated me with respect and made me laugh almost every time we interacted. I found myself asking the front desk attendant what nights he was going to be working, and then intentionally doing my laundry when I knew he would be there. It was an opportunity to walk past the desk to get change for the washer and dryer, flash a smile his way, and strike up a conversation.

Around the same time, I started to notice that Bob visited his sister on my floor more and more often. I figured they either had a really great relationship, or else he kind of liked me. I began intentionally leaving my door open whenever I was in my room, giving him plenty of opportunities to stop by.

On Valentine's Day of my sophomore year, Bob asked me on our first official date. And just like that, we were a couple. He treated me the way I had been yearning to be treated, and helped me remember all that I had to offer. I began to heal and grow whole once more in Bob's arms, seeing myself through his eyes. He graduated and moved back to Denver a year and a half later, just as I was entering my senior year. The distance made things difficult, but we endured, and on New Year's Eve of that year, Bob got down on one knee and asked me to be his wife.

Eight months later, we said our "I Do's."

Now our happily-ever-after life could begin...or so we thought.

Chapter Three

$\mathcal{W}$HEN I THINK back on our first several years of marriage, and how afraid I was of getting pregnant, I can't help but laugh. Oh the irony, given what was to come. But at the time, I just couldn't imagine us adding a third person to our newlywed lifestyle. We were young and just starting out in the world. I wanted so desperately to preserve that moment in our lives. Kids could come later, once we were more established and settled. Surely we had plenty of time.

Bob got a job working for a company in downtown Denver, while I fought to put my degree in education to good use. I couldn't get a full-time teaching position right out of school, so I took on substitute teaching for a while instead. The adorable and clever students renamed me Mrs. O'Toolebox, Mrs. O'Hammer, Four Eyes, and a few other gems not worth mentioning. I loved teaching band and making music with kids, but I didn't love when they all switched instruments and pretended they didn't speak English.

Our first apartment was right across the street from the bus stop. Because I never knew where I would be teaching from day to day, I was the lucky one who got to use our rusted Chevy Citation, purchased from Bob's brother and sister-in-law. This left Bob riding the city bus to and from his office job most days. He waited for that bus in rain, sleet, hail, and snow, with his thermos full of hot soup for lunch, never complaining or acting in any way frustrated by our arrangement. It continued this way for four years, even after he took on evening classes geared towards earning his graduate degree.

One snowy day, I got called for an afternoon teaching assignment. I said an early goodbye to Bob when he left for work, and then set about slowly getting myself ready. He returned an hour later, soaking wet, somehow still with a smile on his face. "I have a very sad story to tell you," he said. "I waited for a bus that never came, then I fell down the hill and got sprayed by all the cars driving through the slush." Looking at him for a second, and realizing he was serious and laughing at the same time, I felt my own laughter bubble up at his expense.

We may not have had material wealth, but we sure enjoyed life and each other.

The next fall, I landed a job teaching elementary school band and orchestra at three separate schools. Bob endured three concerts featuring different children, all playing the same beginning level music. After each one, he acted as though he had just witnessed the Philharmonic.

We relished the simplicity of our lives. Even with busy schedules we both found fulfillment in friends and in each other.

Every so often my period was late and I would panic for a day or two. But then it would arrive, and we would have a good laugh and go on with our modest lives.

After a few years of marriage, however, we really started thinking about having children. We didn't try too hard at first—we just didn't really do anything to *prevent* pregnancy. After a year or so, we started investing a bit more effort—reading up on methods for increasing fertility, tracking my cycle, and timing all the fun stuff. At that point, I was sure it would happen any day.

But instead, another year passed by and we began to worry that something may be wrong. My family physician sent me to a specialist for some unpleasant tests, but they didn't find anything obviously amiss. "Just keep trying," they said. "It will happen eventually," they promised.

Several months later I developed an ovarian cyst, for which the doctor prescribed birth control pills. I gave him a puzzled look and said, "Isn't that a bit counterproductive, when trying to get pregnant?"

"Well yes, ma'am," he responded. "But this cyst needs to go away." I spent another three months waiting for that tiny little cyst that never bothered me at all to go wherever it is that cysts go. And then I waited another two moths for the pills to clear out of my system.

Finally the doctor proclaimed we could begin "trying" to have a child. We negotiated through a few rounds of artificial insemination—the procedure with the horrible name. It adequately described the process that should have provided intimacy to a couple as they made a baby, but instead became sterile and impersonal.

But it was worth it, because in August, I finally became pregnant.

We invited my parents over for dinner and hung baby booties on the doorknocker to announce our news. Everyone rejoiced with us, because they had watched and shared in our heartache over the previous several years. The first doctor's appointment went as expected. I needed monitoring because of a low progesterone level, but everything else seemed to be developing appropriately.

I scheduled the appointment to hear the baby's heartbeat a few weeks later. Waiting for that day felt like an eternity. We were just so excited to hear that gorgeous sound. The day of our appointment though, the technician came in and secured the heart rate monitor on my belly and we all listened. She moved it around a bit, and then some more, and more again.

Nothing.

She assured me the doctor would be able to find it. The doctor came in and hooked me up to an ultrasound monitor. I saw the baby, so I thought everything would be alright, but the look on his face told me a different story. The technician informed us that the baby's measurements showed I wasn't as far along as we had thought.

"You performed the procedure," I pleaded. "The date is in my chart."

The news extinguished my mirage. The doctor told me things like this happened a lot. What he didn't understand was that they didn't happen to me. I had no point of reference for this. Instead of hearing my baby's heartbeat, I needed to have a dilation and curettage (D&C). It was essentially a procedure to remove whatever remnants of what had been my baby from my body, wiping the slate clean, pretending as though it had never happened at all.

Reality invaded my hopes and dreams, and I didn't want to deal with this inevitability right then. But the teaching position I had held at the high school at the time required me to run band camp starting three days later. I didn't have the luxury of thinking about this D&C decision for a few days. Even though I knew my baby was dead, my gut and my mind battled with images of abortion.

Maybe the doctor had made a mistake?

If left alone, perhaps the baby would grow and be fine?

But deep down, I knew. My baby had died, along with my dream.

The nurse took me to a room and asked me to lie down. She started an IV in my hand and gave me some hallucinogenic medication. I complained about the stripes on the wallpaper making me dizzy. "If they bother you," she responded, "don't look at them, sweetie."

To this day, that exchange is still all I remember from the actual procedure, other than the instructions to stay off my feet and out of the sun for the next several days. Everything else is a blur.

Three days later, I stood on a football field for 10 hours in the hot sun, 100 band kids flanking me on either side. They didn't know anything about my ordeal. I pretended as though everything was just fine.

It was the only way I knew how to survive.

Chapter Four

*T*HE ONLY WAY I could avoid plunging into depression was jumping right back into the baby-making pressure cooker. After waiting to heal physically from the D&C, we started the process of trying to get pregnant immediately.

I became obsessed.

I spent all of my non-teaching time working toward this goal. I had always believed that if I worked hard enough at something, I could achieve it. I saw no reason why this issue should be any different. My single-sighted focus certainly put a strain on our physical relationship though, even further stripping the intimacy from our lives and turning those moments that had previously been so pleasurable into part of a no-nonsense quest for the ultimate prize.

I found myself still struggling over the loss of our baby, so we joined a grief support group at the hospital. The other couples had all lost live babies, which left us wondering if we should even be in the group at all. But after we got to know the other couples and shared stories, they welcomed us with open arms. We had much in common and discovered a shared compassion for each other. This had been our only baby and we didn't know if we would ever be able to have another. They all had children and believed they could get pregnant again.

Different stories, different losses, but a bond somehow uniting us as parents of loss nonetheless.

Their grace toward us came as an amazing gift. They showed us that grief is grief, no matter the cause. No one ever got caught up in who had lost more. We had all lost. And that was enough.

Toward the end of that year, our insurance company informed us that we were approaching the expiration of lifetime benefits for infertility treatment. We only had six months remaining, after which point we would lose all access to those benefits. We approached our doctor and told him it was time to pull out the big guns. "Do whatever you've got to do," we said. This felt like our last chance.

He explained a procedure called GIFT, or Gamete Intra-Fallopian Transfer. That certainly sounded important and promising. They would put me on high-powered fertility drugs that would cause me to produce a large number of eggs. Then they would fertilize the eggs and transfer them directly into my fallopian tubes. This was believed to have a higher rate of success than in-vitro fertilization, which involves transfer directly into the uterus, because the embryo traveled a more "natural" pathway.

None of it seemed all that natural to me. But what did I know? I wasn't the one who had attended medical school.

For several weeks I gave myself injections in the thigh daily. Every few days, I bounced to the doctor before school. Having never been a morning person, this proved how far I was willing to go for a baby. They did ultrasounds at each appointment to check on my developing eggs. They seemed to be growing nicely, along with my belly. My stomach had bloated with the fluid retention of 32 potential babies-to-be, making me now look pregnant. A few days before the big science experiment, Bob had to give me several injections in the rear end—a final round of humiliation and indignity in the baby-making journey that had now become completely devoid of sexiness or fun.

Our GIFT day arrived and we went to the hospital for the retrieval process. My 32 eggs impressed even the doctors, a number that apparently was quite large. What can I say? I have always been a bit competitive.

While I recovered after retrieval, those eggs were combined with Bob's sperm in a lab. We sat at home, anxiously waiting to hear the fate of our little babies-to-be. An appointment for transfer was set for the next day at 11:00 am, but we had been told not to go to the hospital until receiving a call from the clinic first. I didn't understand that initially. There had been so many eggs and we knew exactly how long it took to drive to the hospital. But still, we waited for that call.

As the clock ticked 10:30 and then 10:45, I started to get nervous. Why hadn't they called? Why couldn't we just go?

We were going to be late for the appointment! Late for our babies!

A few minutes before 11:00, the phone finally rang. A somber voice on the other end of the line told us to stay home. None of our eggs had fertilized. All 32 were gone.

It was over.

I hung up the phone, a numbness taking over. I had never considered the possibility of this outcome. We had done everything right. Everything we had been told to do. *If I just did what I was supposed to do, things would work out.*

Suddenly, that belief was shattered, my entire world concept crumbling at my feet.

I had used my spring break from teaching to undergo this treatment, but I could not bring myself to face reality when the time came. I took an extra week off to grieve the loss of our baby from the summer before and the baby or babies who would now never be. Our insurance benefits had officially run out.

We had no baby. No insurance. And a bank account that was now completely depleted by our exhaustive efforts.

And it had all been for nothing.

Chapter Five

*A*LIFETIME OF EVENTS played out over the next few weeks. After the failed GIFT procedure, I was desperate to be doing *something*. So I called my dad, a clergyman with plenty of connections. He knew Bob and I were open to adoption and he put us in touch with the owner of an agency.

During our very first conversation, she asked if we would be willing to adopt twins. A woman had come into the agency recently looking for adoptive parents for her babies, who were due in just a few short months. There was a possibility the children were going to be bi-racial and there were some potential complications, including the fact that she couldn't identify the father and she had used drugs during her pregnancy.

This was different from how we had always planned on becoming parents, but we talked at length about the possibility, and then turned the choice over to prayer. My mom suggested we "give God an ultimatum," like Gideon in The Bible, from Judges 6–8:

God used an angel to ask Gideon to rescue Israel from the Midianites. Gideon felt weak, and unable to perform this task. He asked God for a sign to prove he heard correctly. The angel had Gideon prepare a meal and set it on a rock. Then the angel touched the meal with his staff and fire consumed it all. Gideon still doubted, so he asked God to prove His trustworthiness. Gideon placed some wool on the threshing floor at night. "If the fleece is wet with dew in the morning but the ground is dry, then I will know that you are going to help me rescue Israel as you promised." It happened that way, but Gideon still wanted more proof. He asked again, "This time let the fleece remain dry while the ground around it is wet with dew." Again God did what Gideon asked, finally convincing Gideon.

I had never personally felt the need to ask for proof from God before, and I didn't even know that I could. But my mom had always seemed like she knew God pretty well, with a faith that had always felt so unwavering, so we gave it a try. We told God that we could not handle the disappointment if this mother agreed to the adoption and then changed her mind. We had heard so many sad stories of couples preparing for the birth of a child, only to go home empty-handed, and we knew that would be a heartbreak we couldn't overcome.

So we reminded God that we had already suffered loss, just in case He had forgotten. Then we gave Him a week to guide us with an answer. If the week went by and nothing had changed, we would adopt the twins. If He didn't want us to adopt those babies though, He needed to do something to make that clear to us—something He knew I could not fix, because by that point I had come to realize that if I could move mountains to have these babies be mine, I would.

God knew that to be true as well.

On the morning of the last day of our "agreement" with God, nothing had changed. I drove a van filled with my jazz band students to a festival in Greeley, Colorado. We had a great day and I told the kids about our plans to adopt. They were almost as excited as I was. They played well and I floated on cloud nine. I couldn't wait to get home to start planning.

Twins!

We were going to become an instant family!

I arrived home later than usual that day because of the trip to Greeley. Bob was waiting for me at the door. His face was ashen with grief. "The agency called," he said somberly. "They hadn't told the mom they had chosen us as her match, because it wasn't final yet. She called them this afternoon and left a message on their machine saying she was moving back to her home state and would be selecting a new agency there. She's already gone. They have no forwarding number and they don't even know what state she is moving to. It's over. The twins can't be ours."

The familiar feeling of dreams leaving my heart overtook me once again. I could only cry. I knew my prayer had been answered, but in my naivety, I had allowed myself to believe that prayers were only supposed to be answered in the affirmative. If I took the time to pray and include God, why didn't He give me what I wanted? I truly didn't understand.

I found I could relieve my grief somewhat by crying. A lot. We had moved into our first house as we prepared for children to join our family. The empty room next to ours was waiting for our baby. Every time I walked past it, my heart ached.

By this point, it felt like so many babies had come and gone who could have filled that room. Babies *should* have filled that room. But still, it sat empty. The floor of that space became my home, as I sat there night after night, hand sanding the rungs on a used crib, tears streaming down my face. I thought maybe by the time I finished, a baby would appear, filling not just this empty space, but also the hole in my heart.

What a pathetic image. I watched a small TV on the floor in my grubby shorts, with a mask over my face to keep out the dust and tears as I sanded. It was this determination I felt once more to at least be doing *something*…

I actually needed an electric sander and many helping hands to finish off a room that would soon house our very first child.

Chapter Six

*T*HERE WAS A ministry in our town dedicated to helping pregnant teenage girls who had been kicked out by their families. My dad was on the board of directors. They provided the young women with up to two years of housing, parenting classes, education, and job training. Many of them came with nothing and left with a life. Sometimes they chose to parent their children after they learned the skills and had the resources necessary to do so, and sometimes they chose to place their children for adoption. This was not an organization that provided adoption services though. It simply provided the resources to help these women travel whichever path they chose.

I don't know why I called the organization's founder, but after we lost the twins, I thought Sue might offer compassion for my loss. She showed such kindness as I told her all we had been through. She even listened to my tears, and her empathetic voice reminded me that my pain mattered.

At the end of our conversation, she told me about her goddaughter. Sue's family had been hosting sixteen-year-old Lisa for a few months now. Lisa had asked to come stay with them when she found out she was pregnant during the second semester of her junior year in high school. She lived in a small town and hadn't wanted to deal with the gossip of everyone knowing about her condition.

An adoptive family had already been chosen for the baby, but the prospective mother had become severely ill and the family had decided they needed to pull out of the adoption process. With less than two months until Lisa's due date, she was now scrambling to find new parents for her baby.

Sue asked if I would like her to show Lisa our profile and see if she would be interested in meeting us. It felt like a trick question. I had called Sue seeking only compassion for all the lost babies I was now mourning, and here she was, opening up the possibility of another child. Lisa could look at our file and reject us, of course, but…she also might want to meet us. We knew the risk we faced. My heart didn't care; there was no hesitation when I gave her permission to proceed.

We met the beautiful, kind, gentle, honest, sweet, serious, and funny mother-to-be less than a month later. Lisa attended a local high school and was concerned about keeping her secret from classmates. Her pregnant belly looked small, covered by large shirts and a teenager's way of carrying herself, books often low and in front of her as she hunched forward and avoided eye contact. For the most part, people left her alone, much to her relief.

Back home, only her parents and sister knew about the pregnancy. The rest of her extended family and friends believed she had left simply to spend time with her godmother and attend school nearby for a semester. She would return to her hometown for her senior year.

It felt strange to both Bob and me to have a teenager in the position of qualifying us as parents. But Lisa's determination for her child fueled our discussion. She liked our height and hair color, stating that our features reminded her of her and the baby's biological father. She thought that might make it easier for her baby to feel as though he fit into our family.

Lisa also wanted to make certain we would take him to church, which was a given anyway and something we were happy to comply with. She wanted to know that we would start a college fund for her little boy, telling us how her dad had saved $100 for college every month since her birth. That was why she was making the decision she now was; she did not want to disappoint him. She had plans to finish high school and college. She wanted to know her child would have the same opportunities. And she wanted to know that he would have two parents prepared for the challenge of raising a little boy.

Her concern for this baby was palpable, and it was so obvious she did not take this decision lightly. She told us that when she was in sixth grade, her teacher had started the process of adopting a baby, only to have the biological mother change her mind. Lisa had observed her heartbroken teacher, and she assured us that she had made up her mind and would not change it. She was determined not to cause that kind of devastation for any family. I remember being struck by how mature it was of her to even think about us in this process. And there was relief simply in hearing her words.

We attempted to temper our own emotions, not wanting to get hurt again, but…everything about this felt right. We really liked her, everything about her. As we said goodbye, Lisa told us she would let us know of her decision soon, and we silently prayed for this to be our turn.

Bob and I tried to go back to life as normal, whatever that meant. We worked. I sanded. We tried to have fun now and then, but life felt heavy. There had been so much loss and so many failed attempts in such a short period of time. I was overwhelmed by my own grief, and desperate for good news to provide a salve for the wounds.

All around me, everyone was having babies. I was forever feeling accosted by pregnant bellies. I went to several baby showers and always ended up in the bathroom crying. It became too much to handle. I felt happy for my friends who were able to conceive, and I didn't want to seem selfish, but my heart broke for the baby we didn't have. My arms ached to hold an infant of my own. I remember thinking that I didn't care where that baby came from, just so long as it could truly be ours. I knew I would love any child I was blessed with.

Mother's Day rolled around, and we still had not heard from Lisa. Weeks had gone by. We knew she was due in five weeks, and wondered if she had found another couple. Were we not good enough? Did she not like us? This day that was already filled with so much sadness for me now felt even heavier. What if I never became a mother? What if we just never received the blessing I had been praying so long for?

It was 8:00 that night when the phone rang, Lisa's voice on the other end of the line catching me off guard. "I just wanted to wish you a Happy Mother's Day," she said. "And to tell you that you are going to be a mother. If you still want to be?"

I burst into tears and just said, "Thank you!" over and over again. I spent the rest of that evening parading through our phone directory and announcing the news to everyone we knew.

We were going to be parents!

Our waiting ended and preparation began in earnest. We immediately bought an electric sander and got to work on the crib. A friend took over sanding the changing table, because I couldn't finish them both in time. And then I started in on the paperwork. I had never been very good at completing mounds of paperwork like what was required. I remember thinking in college that I appreciated the life of a music major because my tests included analyzing notes, not writing papers. There was nothing about writing that I enjoyed, and attempting to gather so much information and organize it intimidated me to no end. But the adoption came at us so quickly, I didn't even have time to get nervous about the paperwork. I just did it.

Shelley planned a baby shower for my last day of school, which seemed like perfect timing because it was going to leave us with two weeks to prepare for our little boy's arrival. Except that the day before the shower was meant to happen, as Bob attended a business meeting in New Orleans, I received a phone call from Sue. She was calling to notify me that they were taking Lisa to the hospital due to low amniotic fluid. The doctor would induce labor in the morning. Cell phones didn't exist back then, so I called Bob's hotel and left the following message for him: "Come home now, your baby is about to be born!" He immediately scheduled the earliest flight available, the next morning.

I made my way to school the next day and called the hospital in between each class. It felt pointless to even be there on this last day, where nothing much is accomplished. Our concerts were all finished and my students had already checked out. I had as well—my heart and mind there in that hospital room where I could not be. My fellow faculty members put a board in the lounge stating the increase in "my" dilation and the time between "my" contractions. I laughed, but wanted desperately just to leave. Because of our shortened schedule, and my lack of a final class, I bolted from the school around 11:00 am.

My mom made her way to our apartment after picking up Bob from the airport. We met at home just before noon and headed to the hospital together. Bob and I discussed whether we should stop for lunch or go straight there. We didn't know Lisa's family and didn't want our presence to make this harder on any of them, but we were also so excited. We decided to go to the hospital, check in, and then get something to eat. When I had called earlier, the nurse had informed me that Lisa hadn't made much progress and that this might be an all-day event, but I still wanted to stop by—just to give our support.

We arrived at the hospital just before 1:00 in the afternoon, proceeding straight to the nurse's station. As we neared the desk, we heard the screams of a woman struggling to bring life into the world. My heart tugged at each and every one of her screams. We inquired about Lisa's room number and the nurse immediately blocked us from entering. Those screams were coming from Lisa! Her mom, dad, and boyfriend had all left for lunch less than a half hour before, and she had quickly progressed to 10 centimeters while on her own. We stood behind her door as outsiders, stepping aside when her family arrived and raced to her aid.

For a brief moment, we felt totally out of place. We were the parents, but relegated to the hallway. Concern obviously needed to be focused on Lisa, and we understood that, but the situation illuminated the peculiarity of adoption.

It was only a few minutes later when we heard a different kind of cry—a baby's cry. Our son had arrived.

We endured the hallway, glancing nervously at each other. Was any of this real? Our son had been born, but we felt completely detached from the situation. The minutes passed by like hours, until finally the door opened and the nurse asked if we would like to come in and hold our son.

As we entered the room, we heard the doctor ask Lisa if she wanted to hold him. She responded by asking if we had arrived yet, stating that she wanted his parents to be the first to have that honor. She had no idea the gift she gave her son and us at that moment, and the more I've learned about attachment bonds in the last two decades, the more valuable I have come to believe those moments were.

We stepped into the room and the nurse handed our son to us for the very first time. The scene was surreal: the doctor stitching Lisa as we held her child, everyone in the room (doctors and nurses included) crying at the beauty, pain, and happiness all tied into this incredible moment.

The rest of the day we were privileged to be able to experience his first bath, first feeding, shots, and everything else a newborn endures in those first hours of life. Because I had not delivered him myself, I was allowed to attend all of those firsts that most mothers miss. I took each event in with astonishment and awe. The hospital staff let us spend private time with our baby in an empty room. Their kindness proved they understood our role in this adventure. We needed the time for us, but also didn't want to interfere with Lisa and her family, and the grief they must surely now be feeling.

Late in the day, I remembered the baby shower that had been planned for that evening. We decided I should still try to attend, so Bob dropped me off at my sister's house for my own baby shower, armed with pictures of my new baby boy. Because I had already seen and held him, each gift meant that much more. I found myself clinging particularly to a hand-sewn blanket created by a good friend. A soft bunny covered most of the fabric, with protruding ears and feet for little hands to grasp. I was immediately drawn to it.

Little did I know, that blanket would never leave my son's side. It quickly became his favorite as well.

Thinking we had two weeks to prepare for our baby's birth after school got out, we had not yet chosen his name.

We had hoped to bring our nameless boy home from the hospital the day after his birth, but they would not release him until his birth mother was ready to go home herself. Lisa had suffered from back labor and needed to stay an extra day.

My dad planned a service for both families in the hospital chapel. This beautiful time honored each person, and the role they played in our little boy's existence. We were all touched by this celebration of life.

Lisa gave us two gifts for the baby. The first was a handkerchief to wear on his head at his baptism and in his pocket on his wedding day. It came with this poem, author unknown:

I'm just a little hanky
As square as square can be,
But with a stitch or two,
A bonnet was made of me.
I'll be worn from the hospital
Or on the Christening day.
Then I'll be carefully pressed,
And neatly packed away.
For her Wedding Day,
So we've been told
Every well-dressed bride,
Must have that something very old.
So what could be more fitting,
Than to unpack little me.
And with the stitches snipped,
A hanky I will be.
And if perchance it is a boy,
Someday he'll surely wed.
So to his bride, he can present
The hanky once worn upon his head.

The other gift was a poem we framed and hung in his nursery:

Legacy of an Adopted Child, author unknown:

Once there were two women who never knew each other;
One you do not remember, the other you call Mother.
Two different lives, shaped to make yours one;
One became your guiding star, the other became your sun.
The first gave you life, and the second taught you to live it.
One gave you a nationality, the other gave you a name.
One gave you the seed of talent, the other gave you an aim.
One gave you emotions, the other calmed your fears.
One saw your first sweet smile, the other dried your tears.

> *One gave you away—it was all she could do.*
> *The other prayed for a child, and GOD led her straight to you.*
> *And now you ask, through your tears,*
> *the age-old question unanswered through the years.*
> *Heredity or Environment—which are you the product of.*
> *Neither my darling, neither. Just two different kinds of love.*

By release day, we had finally decided on the name Brendan Nicholas O'Toole. After watching the hospital videos on how to feed and change a baby, we were all permitted to leave our hospital bubble and enter the world in our new roles. Lisa held Brendan as they wheeled her to the front of the facility. She wanted to watch us buckle him into his car seat and make sure he was safe. We complied with her wishes, and then said a tearful goodbye before driving away.

It was then that our emotions again took us by surprise. It felt as if we were kidnapping someone else's child. We kept checking the rearview mirror for the police officer that might pull us over and arrest us any minute. It couldn't possibly be this easy, could it? After everything else we had endured, could we finally have our happy ending?

We arrived home in total silence. We didn't know what to do next. At the hospital, the nurses had been around to tell us when to feed and change Brendan. Now our doorway replaced the hospital hallway, and we still felt out of place and totally unprepared for this new adventure.

Lisa's mom had given us a suggestion about what to do when we arrived home. "Get undressed and snuggle together in bed." She told us it would be soothing for us all, and that it would allow our little boy to start becoming accustomed to our smell and warmth, recognizing it as his own safe place now. We were so physically and emotionally exhausted from the last few days, we wound up doing exactly that. We fell asleep immediately.

After all the commotion to finish his room, Brendan didn't sleep in it for months. We placed him in his crib, but he looked so tiny, and his room seemed so far away. After waiting so long for him, I simply wasn't prepared to have him in another room. So because we didn't have a bassinet, we placed a soft-sided suitcase at the end of our bed and that became his space for the next few weeks of life.

All of us huddled together in one room—the family I had been yearning for all along.

Chapter Seven

PARENTING BECAME THE greatest thing we had ever experienced. As all new parents soon discover, days would go by without us accomplishing a single thing. We stared at Brendan for hours at a time. Nothing else seemed to register on our radar besides him. We thought, *What did we do all day before we had this child to look at?* Life had changed in an instant. It would never be the same again.

There were noticeable differences between adopting and birthing a child. For one, because I hadn't gone through the physical exertion of delivering a baby, I needed no time to recuperate. When six-pound Brendan reached the milestone of living for one whole week, I stopped by a Subway restaurant to pick up dinner. I was dressed up for some reason, and my outfit revealed a trim figure. A man asked me, "Is that your son?" I answered, "Yes!" and he replied, "Wow, my wife never looked that good after our babies were born." I reveled in the compliment and surreptitiously avoided revealing to him the reality of our situation.

I couldn't breastfeed and Brendan needed a bottle every two hours, morning and night. He ate slowly and it felt like he was eating all the time. If he wasn't eating, we were preparing for him to eat. The amount of time spent on feedings was a bit overwhelming, particularly with so few breaks in between. Nights passed with Bob and me taking turns in the rocking chair, dozing as Brendan sucked on his bottle.

I decided I didn't want to return to teaching that fall, so I took a maternity leave, an option that made me laugh in the face of my inability to get pregnant. My childless friends asked me what I did all day. I simply couldn't describe it to them, but I knew that I was loving every minute I had with my little man. I loved being a mom. It felt like my heart had finally found a reason to exist. Pouring myself into someone else and having him respond to my love gratified me.

The court finalized Brendan's adoption approximately six months after his birth, and our celebratory sigh of relief surely must have rippled across the entire world. We threw a huge party and invited all of our family and friends. We knew that Lisa had promised she would not change her mind, and we trusted her, but having the legalities out of the way lifted a weight off our shoulders we hadn't even entirely realized we were carrying. The law now recognized Brendan as our son, and nothing could ever change that fact.

At the end of that first semester, I decided to go back to school on a limited basis. The administrators agreed to allow me to teach four classes instead of the usual five. I taught periods one through four without a planning period or lunch break. That way, I only needed to find someone to babysit until about noon each day. There were several evenings when I had to return to school for a meeting, rehearsal, or concert, but Bob was always available to stay with Brendan during those events.

There were a lot of benefits to being back at school, and I loved the students and the music. But I quickly grew frustrated knowing that Brendan stayed up all morning while I taught, only to need a nap as soon as I got home. It felt like other people were getting to enjoy him at his best, while I could only watch him sleep.

Our first holiday that year landed on Martin Luther King, Jr. Day. School had only been back in session for about two weeks, but I was ready for the break. I woke up that morning with a strange thought; I suddenly couldn't remember the last time I had had my period.

I thought about it for a while. I had been so used to tracking my cycle and calculating events, that the freedom of letting go after Brendan's birth seemed amazing. I hadn't thought about that part of my life for a while now, and it felt good to not have it ruling my world. But that morning, I couldn't for the life of me remember when I had last cycled.

I called Bob at work and asked if he remembered. He didn't know either. I started to get a weird feeling. We both recalled the night of Brendan's adoption party, the margarita that had made me a bit tipsy, and the joy of a marriage without pressure or schedules.

More than six weeks had passed since then.

Could it be? Bob told me to go to the pharmacy and buy a pregnancy test. I should have bought stock in one of those companies years before, but now I no longer had any on hand. I had given up on those tests—they never worked right, as far as I was concerned. I had a gut feeling this time might be different, though. I packed up Brendan and headed out in the Colorado cold to the pharmacy. Upon returning home, I took the test and waited anxiously as I had done so many times before.

The stick turned blue, but I couldn't remember what that meant. I re-read the instructions and looked back at the test several times, feeling suddenly unable to comprehend English. It couldn't be. We had tried for years to conceive and nothing had ever worked. Now we had our baby and I'd gotten pregnant without even "trying?"

We were such an adoption cliché, just like the old wives' tale that once people stop trying to have a baby, they will finally get pregnant.

I called Bob and told him the results. He suggested I go to the doctor for confirmation. I received the same answer there that I had received at home. Pregnant. Once again, my progesterone levels were low, so they put me on a schedule for progesterone shots three times a week. I now had a six-month-old baby, I had just retuned to work, and I was six weeks pregnant.

Shock was all that could register.

After racing to Bob's office to share the news, I returned home, only to realize I had been all over town with my sweater on inside out and backwards. The tag hung right below my chin, yet no one had said a word.

The reaction from family and friends to this pregnancy felt distinctly different from the first one. No one appeared happy for me. They were all concerned that I would get part way into the pregnancy and lose the baby again. I knew they were trying to keep me from an emotional fall, but it really hurt to have no one willing to express any kind of joy. I felt like I was going through this pregnancy alone.

Once the shock faded, I was overcome by excitement. I absolutely loved Brendan and being a mom, and now I had the chance to experience pregnancy and deliver a baby. It made me sad that so many around us were so afraid of loss that they wouldn't celebrate the potential joy of this pregnancy, but I refused to allow that to dilute my own happiness. I went to every doctor's appointment with anticipation and excitement. My hormone levels climbed normally with the help of the progesterone and everything seemed to be proceeding as it should.

After my first trimester, I didn't need the shots anymore, but I was still considered a "high-risk" pregnancy. This turned out to be an unexpected bonus. I got to have more ultrasounds than most pregnant women and I so loved seeing those photos. It was the early '90s, so the pictures were nothing like the 3D images available today, but they were still glimpses of *our* baby. The doctor knew the baby's gender and asked if I wanted to know as well. I absolutely did! In his words, "I'm pretty sure it's a girl, so go ahead and buy lots of pink, but save the receipts just in case!"

I could now spend the months that remained getting to know her, talking to her, and imagining her sweet face.

We started thinking of names as soon as we heard she would be a girl. The weeks surrounding Brendan's arrival had felt so stressful, adding a ton of pressure to the naming of our little boy. But this seemed different, because we had plenty of time to get to know our daughter, Katie Elizabeth O'Toole.

I talked to her all the time, rubbing my belly and singing to her as she bounced around inside me. I taught high school band and orchestra, so she was exposed to a huge dose of music before her birth—a fact that I still believe contributed to her own eventual love of music. The fact that I gave into the craving for hot fudge Sundays nearly every afternoon of my pregnancy may also have contributed to her equal adoration for ice cream!

My job required me to be on my feet all day and my students demanded a lot of energy, so by the time I got home most days, I was ready to collapse. The last part of my pregnancy passed by without any drama, which brought such relief. I gained quite a bit of weight and had a hard time breathing when doing anything physical, which included walking up the stairs and carrying Brendan. But otherwise, I felt pretty good.

Of course, it was also summer and I felt like a blimp, not doing much beyond sitting on the couch trying not to melt in the absence of air conditioning. I normally loved summer, but the extra weight made me so hot. Only September brought relief.

As my due date drew closer, the doctor kept track of Katie's weight as well as mine. He thought she would be over eight pounds at birth, so he didn't want me to go past my due date. At one point, he suggested I might be two weeks further along than I had originally thought because of her measurements, but late in the pregnancy, they decided the initial due date was probably accurate.

I had gotten it in my head that I would deliver two weeks early, so after that date passed, I felt overdue. By that point, I was ready for this miraculous pregnancy I had so long hoped for to come to an end. I cried almost daily and I truly believed I might be the only woman in the world to never deliver her baby. I pictured myself living as a pregnant woman the rest of my life, Katie growing larger and older inside of me. I sobbed at my final three appointments.

Finally, on the day before my due date at my regular appointment, my doctor asked when I would like to deliver. I hadn't experienced contractions yet, but he was worried that Katie might grow too big to deliver vaginally. Through my tears, I responded with, "NOW!" He told me to go home and eat some chicken broth and a piece of plain toast, and then promised to meet me at the hospital that afternoon.

We were going to have a baby!

Chapter Eight

*I*T WAS A little after three in the afternoon when we arrived at the hospital. They started me on a drug to induce labor shortly after we walked in the door, but I was allowed to continue pacing the halls for a few hours as the contractions got going. I did this only because I knew it would get things moving along, not because it was comfortable to do so. In fact, the induction medications caused strong contractions right from the start, leaving me struggling and holding onto the walls as they hit.

Bob got the idea from our birthing class that labor would involve me tucked away in a hospital bed as he coached me through the contractions with soothing breathing exercises. After a few hours of this pained walking and gasping for air whenever another contraction came on, he hesitated before asking when the breathing exercises would start. I harshly spat back, "What do you think I've been doing for the past several hours?"

Around 10:30 p.m., I was given another round of medication for the pain. This time a drug-induced silliness came over me, and I laughed until I cried while watching Late Night with David Letterman.

I stole only a few catnaps that evening, begging for an epidural somewhere in the early morning hours. Just before dawn, I was told that my contractions weren't regular enough, and so they made me wait. The doctor came in and broke my water at 9:00 am, and only then did things start progressing. Finally, they allowed me to have that epidural I had requested hours before. It wasn't what I had been expecting though. I wavered between not being able to feel anything at all, and still feeling almost everything.

They had to keep adjusting the dosage in the drip line, attempting to find the amount that would be right for my body. It seemed like it all should have been simpler than that, but no—apparently pain management isn't an exact science.

Shortly after noon, they instructed me to start pushing. After two and a half hours, the doctor debated taking me in for an emergency C-section. Because of Katie's head size, and my exhaustion, I was struggling to get her out. But I really hated the idea of having surgery after all that time spent in labor. I asked for just 30 more minutes, and I started pushing once more.

Just when I was about to give up, my mom grabbed my hand and put it on Katie's head. I felt her hair and knew that I could do this. It was that moment of being so close that gave me the courage and strength to finally push her out. Katie arrived into the world at 3:10 pm, precisely on her due date. She exceeded the doctor's prediction of eight pounds, and weighed in at 9 pounds 14 ounces. She was 21 inches long.

Physically drained, I couldn't even hold her for very long once she was finally in my arms. I was too afraid I was going to drop her; I simply had no strength left.

I desperately needed food. I kept asking the nurses to bring me something to eat, but dinner didn't arrive until 6:00 p.m. I circled everything on the menu, thinking I would share with Bob, but I wound up eating everything they brought. I had never been so famished.

Friends came by the hospital later that night and thoughtfully brought a pizza, so Bob was able to have a meal after all. I ate some of that as well. But as my friends sat around laughing in celebration, I found that my own laughter was too painful to bear. My body just couldn't handle the ruckus yet, and I had to ask everyone to leave.

Throughout the night, a nurse would bring Katie to me for a feeding every few hours. During one of those visits, she laughed as she checked our wristbands against one another. "I don't really need to check this one." She said. "All the other babies are five or six pounders. But your daughter's practically sitting up and looking around. We're not going to mistake her with another baby."

It was during one of those rare moments alone that I stretched Katie out along the side of my body to look at her. Her head lined up under my armpit and she stretched all the way down to my knees. I stared in awe as I thought about the miracle that had just occurred. I tried to imagine her stuffed back up inside my body, picturing how she would have had to bend and squish to fit. The reality of this miracle I had been blessed to participate in overwhelmed me.

We took Katie home from the hospital on her third day of life. She had jaundice, so she had to spend all of her time in a suitcase with fluorescent lights. Her yellow skin indicated a high bilirubin level and the doctor worried about her liver function. I struggled with this turn of events. I loved being a mother, and in a very short period of time I had been gifted with two beautiful children, but I couldn't hold her yet. Everything about that made me ache.

Hour after hour, she had to stay under those lights. They made her sleepy, so I couldn't even enjoy the alert moments I had experienced with Brendan. She had a "singed hair" smell to her skin, rather than the sweet little baby smell I had grown so used to the first time around. She slept in the same room, yet I could not pick her up and snuggle her except for feedings. I dragged out the feeding times, yearning for as much physical contact as I could get.

Both of our children started out their lives with us by sleeping in suitcases.

Finally, after three days of torture being kept physically at arm's length from my newborn, we were told she could be moved from the suitcase, given a bath, and begin her normal life.

It was then that we were able to experience the joy of Brendan falling in love with his little sister. He held and kissed her every chance he got, never exhibiting any signs of sibling rivalry. And we settled into our happy life as a family of four, with two babies who had been so very wanted and loved now by our sides.

We had our family.

Two children only 15 months apart led to a life of diapers and double everything: cars seats, cribs, high chairs, a double stroller, and one tired mama. It was the life I had always wanted, and I cherished every tired moment.

The thought of leaving the kids in someone else's care was unthinkable after all we had been through to have our family. We made the decision for me start a home-based business with The Pampered Chef, which turned out to be very successful. This allowed me to quit teaching and stay home with the kids during the day, so I had the best of both worlds.

Chapter Nine

MY PARENTS HAD moved to Arizona soon after Katie was born, so we cherished our warm trips to visit "Nanny and Bampa." We had just been to Arizona visiting my family, and my dad chased after our kids with more energy than either Bob or I had, combined. They absolutely loved their Bampa, and he loved both kids equally, even though he often had Brendan tag along in the car with him for "just us boys' time." He still called Brendan "Menmen"—the name with which my little man anointed himself at two years old. Katie loved swimming in her grandparents' pool, especially when Bampa jumped in and swam the length of the water beneath her. He was such a special man, and our kids adored his gentle spirit.

I received a call shortly after we got home, asking me to fly immediately to Chicago for the weekend in order to sit on a panel for The Pampered Chef. Excitedly, I agreed; no one had ever asked me to do anything like this before! I kissed the kids and Bob "goodbye," never expecting that anything would change so drastically while I was gone.

I landed in Chicago in the late afternoon. As I checked into my hotel, they told me I had an urgent message to call home. My heart began to race as I dialed Bob from my room. He answered the phone, and through his sobs told me that my dad had died that afternoon. I sat in disbelief and shock. How could this have happened? I had just seen him.

He had been out that afternoon with his older brother, Paul, a doctor in Scottsdale, Arizona. They had always been close, but also behaved as you might expect brothers would—competing in nearly everything they did together. That day included a bike ride in the desert. Paul later told me that he had noticed my dad didn't have his usual edge, and asked if he felt okay. Dad stopped his bike and said his chest hurt, so my uncle went into doctor mode and took his pulse. They rested for a time, but Paul knew he needed medical attention quickly.

Paul wanted to call for a helicopter, but didn't want to worry my dad. Dad had a cell phone in his fanny pack, but didn't tell Paul. In retrospect, it was a recipe of could-have's and would-have's—a culmination of if-only's.

Finally, other riders came along their path, and Paul called for emergency help. They needed to get to a clearing where the helicopter could land. My dad told his brother that his chest no longer hurt and that he suddenly felt just fine. I've wondered if God provided him peace just before the end. Paul pushed both bicycles as my dad walked slowly behind him. As my uncle looked back at my father one last time, he watched him drop to the ground.

He believes to this day that my dad died instantly, but he performed rescue breathing and chest compressions for 40 minutes until the flight for life crew arrived. They wanted to shock his heart on the chopper, but he had no electrical activity at all.

My dad was only 57 when he left this earth.

I spent that long night on the phone, alternating between my mom and the airline. I flew straight from Chicago to Phoenix, while Bob drove 14 hours with Brendan and Katie to meet me there. Two of my siblings lived near my parents, and my brother Dave arrived shortly before me. He met me at the plane, and I fell apart in his arms.

We spent a shock-filled week at my mom's house, smiling politely at strangers, accepting gifts of food, and enduring the constant streams of people that accompany a death in the family.

We returned home after the funeral, but the shock remained for several months. I remember pacing my house, not able to grasp the reality of my dad's sudden passing. I experienced strange reactions from some friends. Nobody knew how to react to my grief. It was as if they feared my devastation might rub off on them, so they would say all the wrong things in an attempt to quell their own anxiety.

"God needed an angel." *No. God didn't need anything, He is all-sufficient. People don't turn into angels when they die. And God didn't take my dad away from me and his grandkids just to add to his angel army.*

"He is in a better place." *He may be, but I am not. I miss my dad. You're not helping.*

"It's probably for the best." *Are you kidding me right now?!? My dad is **dead**! How is that for the best for anyone?*

"Maybe it's a blessing in disguise?" *Get out of my face. Right now.*

"Just remember the scripture... all things work together for good to those who love God, to those who are the called according to His purpose (Romans 8:28)." *Great. I get it. I've known this my whole life. But right now? Not the time. You may be making yourself feel better, but my heart is still shredded into a million pieces.*

So many people said these stupid things, thinking they were helping, when really they only made my heartache worse. It wasn't about me and my grief; it was about consoling themselves. And I didn't want to hear it.

The people who actually comforted me?

"I'm so sorry for your loss." *Thank you.*

"I don't even know what to say." *No words, just a much needed hug.*

"This must feel so shocking." *Yes. I'm overwhelmed. And I don't understand.*

"I miss him too." *Thank you. I know he made a difference.*

In the months that followed, we all struggled to put the pieces back together. But my world was rocked in a way I was not sure I would ever recover from. I missed my dad every day.

I felt camaraderie with those who had personally experienced grief, just as I had after the miscarriage. They could relate to my sadness, lack of energy, and desire to talk about my dad. They weren't afraid to bring up the subject, and addressed it head-on. I found myself drawn to these people, to keep me from slipping further into isolation.

Death impacted us all differently, but Brendan's kindergarten teacher noticed a change in his behavior almost immediately. He had trouble settling down, focusing, and staying on task. We later learned that for Brendan, Bampa was the first significant person he knew to die. As with many adopted children, the loss of his birth mother occurred before he could verbalize his sadness and confusion. This death subconsciously triggered the memory of the loss of his biological mother, creating compounded grief.

Chapter Ten

*A*T AGES SEVEN and six, Brendan and Katie simultaneously announced that they wanted a brother. "Not a baby," they explained, "but a ready-to-play brother."

We hadn't even talked about adopting again. Before we got married, we discussed the idea of adopting from Vietnam, since my family had adopted my brother, Dave, from Vietnam when I was a child. I loved my brother dearly, and enjoyed our adoption experience. Once again the subject of adoption was on the table.

Bob and I looked at an adoption website one night, faces of children waiting to be adopted filling our screen and melting our hearts. Their eyes pleaded, *Pick me, pick me!* So many children needed families. But did they need *this* family?

Child Kills Family Cat

Child Sets House on Fire

Child Destroys School Property

Child Suffers from Reactive Attachment Disorder (RAD)

Stories of adoption gone awry had just started making their way into the news, and it was those stories of adopted children tormenting family pets, setting fires, and dividing families that sat just below the surface as

I spoke with the woman from the adoption agency. Brendan's adoption had gone so seamlessly, but we had held him in our arms from birth. There were different concerns at hand when it came to adopting an older child, and while I felt as though we surely had enough love to give, I was afraid of getting in over our heads.

We went to the same agency we used when adopting Brendan and the counselor seemed to understand our concerns. She asked us if race was an issue. It wasn't, so she recommended we think about adopting from Vietnam. "They treat the kids so well there," she told us. "It's just like a family." I remembered being a little girl and thinking that I would one day adopt from Vietnam, and the conversation with Bob before we married…this tapped into that old desire. And so Vietnam entered the forefront of our thoughts. But we didn't make any drastic decisions. It was more something we talked about from time to time, playing with the idea without really doing anything to move forward.

My maternal grandma died two years after my dad. She spent time in the hospital, then an assisted living facility, and then six weeks in a beautiful hospice. I took Brendan and Katie to visit her often, and the hospice staff welcomed them with brownies and movies. During her last few weeks, Bob and I started to think seriously about adopting. The timing seemed strange, but somehow my grandma's death helped us make our decision to adopt. When faced with the end of a life, it caused us to re-evaluate our own lives, and how we wanted to live. We had been blessed, and wanted to share with a child who didn't have much of a future. Brendan's adoption and transition into our family had been wonderful, and we were eager to do it again.

We thought about what the counselor had said about the Vietnamese treating the children like family. She said our risk for dealing with RAD was greatly reduced because the children were loved and treated so well. She assured us that the children coming from Russian-block countries seemed to suffer from attachment issues at a much higher rate. These babies were stacked in cribs along walls of over-crowded orphanages, and they had to figure out how to get milk out of a bottle, on their own, in order to survive.

Vietnam seemed like a great option.

We turned in our application to adopt from Vietnam that May. The paperwork was similar to what we had completed when adopting Brendan, except that the state required more documents, more copies, and more state seals. I obtained them easily, but the extreme amount of paper required and the hoops we had to jump through to complete everything made the process difficult and time consuming.

We had to be persistent, going back to various places repeatedly. Depending so heavily on others for the process to continue advancing was maddening.

All along, we said that we would take things one step at a time, and if it ever got too overwhelming, we would stop. The first contact we had from the agency contained a picture of a two-and-a-half-year-old boy. We saw his age and decided not to look at his picture. We could not reject a little child, but we needed to reject his age. Brendan and Katie were seven and six, and we wanted our new child to be around five. The hope was that they would all be able to play together.

A few months later, another picture arrived. This three-and-a-half-year-old boy caused us to stop and make a decision. If we sent this one back, we might wait months for another child, and that one might be only four—the same age this boy would then be by that time. If this child turned out to be our son, we didn't want him in that orphanage any longer than necessary. We decided to take a leap, choosing him to join our family.

We finally got to see a few pictures. He looked really cute, but a bit scared. I struggled with a strange thought. In most of the pictures, he looked exactly the same, generally content and happy. But in one picture, Katie and I couldn't tell if it was even the same boy. He had a different look on his face and we thought the agency might have made a mistake. This picture showed a boy with a different attitude, and I didn't know if I liked what I saw. But others didn't seem to notice the difference, so I shook off my concern and told myself I was being silly.

The day we decided to adopt this little boy, I had a Pampered Chef party I had to conduct after sending our formal acceptance to the agency. I drove 40 minutes to the show, only to find that in my excitement I had left all of my tools at home in our garage. Luckily, the hostess had been to many shows before and had most of the products I needed. All of the guests understood and celebrated with me. They thought it was cute that my mind had been so focused on my son; I had basically completely forgotten my work. "Mommy brain" they called it already.

Most of our friends and family were happy for us as we prepared for our new family member, but some seemed silent through the process. We discovered that many people had strong feelings about Vietnam, adoption, foreign vs. domestic adoption, and adopting an older child. We received a lot of questions:

"Why Vietnam when there are so many needy children here?"

"Why don't you get a baby, so you can start fresh?"

"Are you sure you know what you are getting into?"

That period of questioning turned out to be enlightening. People thought they were questioning us, but they were actually revealing deep-seated fears of their own. I understood the struggle for people who had lost a loved one in the Vietnam War, those who served in Vietnam personally seemed to battle with the notion, but softened as they thought of a child gaining a family in the United States. The people I struggled with the most were those who were just blatantly racist.

We went to an amusement park in Denver, Colorado, with some friends the summer we waited for our son to join us. It seemed like all of Denver had the same idea. At lunchtime, a large, Hispanic family started their picnic at some tables not too far from the line where we waited. We heard really obnoxious music blasting from a boom box.

Our friends started making comments about how Hispanic families tend to do everything together, and how they like to blast music, not caring how anyone else feels. At first, I thought our friends were just frustrated about the annoying music and horrible lyrics. I loved that this family came to have a picnic at the park. It looked like several generations had all gathered for the day, and what about that could possibly be wrong?

But it wasn't long before I realized that our friends truly had hostile feelings towards these people. I didn't understand. They were at a public table, minding their own business, and not bothering anyone—after all, we couldn't be sure they were the ones responsible for this music. They were actually doing exactly what we were doing, enjoying the day at the amusement park.

The comments continued though, and my face started to get hotter and hotter. I hoped they would just stop. I liked these friends and enjoyed being able to do things together with our families, but I did not like what I heard. After too many comments, I finally blurted out, "Stop it, my son is Hispanic."

Brendan played with the other kids, totally unaware of the comments that were being made, but it didn't matter. We had never made a big deal about his Hispanic origins, not even at his birth, because he had never been anything other than *our son*. But this kind of racism bothered me. Those people had the same right to the amusement park as we did. The idea that our friends had a problem with Hispanics, somehow ignoring completely that our son had Hispanic genes, made me feel ill.

Bob and I took the kids and got out of line to cool off, and it dawned on me that this might be the reason they hadn't asked about our upcoming adoption. Most of our friends were interested and asked about the process often. These friends occasionally offered up a polite question here and there, but didn't really seem to want to know much about our soon-to-be son. If they had problems with Hispanic people, what must they think of us bringing an Asian boy into our family?

I suddenly did not even want to know these people. If they couldn't be accepting of our children, and others like our children, then they were no friends of ours.

This made me wonder how many others in our world would respond to our Vietnamese son with similar contempt—but it was a possibility I had no other choice but to accept. I was not going to let anyone's ignorance and prejudice hinder us from following our hearts' desire to adopt this boy we'd already fallen in love with and dreamt about day and night.

By the way, the music blasted from the boom box of a couple of scary-looking white teenagers.

Chapter Eleven

*B*ECAUSE OUR NEW son lived in a foreign county, and because of his age, we had to participate in special training from the state to finalize our adoption. When we adopted Brendan, we had been required to complete about eight hours of training, but this time, we needed a total of twenty-four. We spent two intense training weekends with other adoptive parents. The training included topics on parenting wounded kids, parenting traumatized children, fetal alcohol syndrome, and how to promote attachment.

As we sat through the session that listed symptoms of an insecure attachment, Bob and I leaned together and said, "This is Brendan." We were there to learn how to bond with the child we didn't yet know, but we found ourselves recognizing many of the symptoms of attachment disorders in the child we had been parenting for years.

Since my dad's death, Brendan had been experiencing some attention and focus issues at school. We learned through this session that trauma can bring out unhealed wounds from early on in a child's life. There was more as well, but we didn't fully understand all of it. So we decided to make an appointment with the psychologist who had been heading the workshop.

Brendan was our son, and we had loved him with our whole hearts since the day we first learned he would be ours. If he was now struggling with his attachment to us, we wanted to do whatever we could to help him, particularly if our new son may also arrive struggling with the same issues, albeit on a larger scale.

Our first appointment with Dr. Fuller took place at his office in Colorado Springs, about an hour from our home, just months after our initial application to adopt from Vietnam. He explained that all adopted children carry with them some wounds. We didn't understand how that could be possible, since Brendan had come into our family at birth and had never attached to anyone else. But Dr. Fuller told us to think of it in the same way as a parent losing a baby. "If you lost a child at birth," he questioned, "how long do you think it would affect you?"

Forever.

According to Dr. Fuller, the same is true for children losing their biological mother through death or adoption.

He explained that Brendan, like all adopted children, had grown inside the womb of his birth mother for nine months. He got to know her walk, talk, smell, and feel. He learned his mother's voice and grew to feel safe with her. Their hearts beat together. When the day of his birth arrived, it should have been a great time of meeting the one he had trusted and known for his entire existence.

Instead, he was handed to a stranger who smelled, walked, talked, and moved different from what he was used to. He didn't understand and had no language skills to express himself, but there was a feeling of, "Huh? This isn't right!"

We understood. I had known the loss of children I'd never met. I knew that pain. I had healed and moved on, but I would never forget. I hadn't realized babies could go through something similar though. But as Dr. Fuller spoke to us, it suddenly all made sense. *Of course* there is a loss there for them. How had I never seen that before? And why was it something that had never been discussed in any of our previous adoption classes?

Brendan's behavior had been growing progressively worse over time, and the school had begun calling us more often. His second grade teacher seemed to really like quiet girls who did what they were told. Brendan was not a girl, and he liked to play hard and talk loud. He had his own mind and lots of ideas that needed to be shared. He didn't like school because of his love for movement and his creative brain. It became about enduring and getting by for him, not learning or exploring. That made my heart ache for my little boy, and I struggled to find a way to help him.

His teacher told me she thought he had Attention Deficit Hyperactivity Disorder (ADHD) and needed to be put on Ritalin. I couldn't wrap my head around that. I knew it would have made *her* life easier, but we cared about his heart and didn't want him to feel that he needed to change. He didn't strike us as a hyperactive boy. He just seemed like a *boy* to us—a bit rough and tumble and all over the place from time to time, but no more so than you would expect from a boy his age. We didn't want to put him on medication, and we didn't want to squash his creativity. He had never received consistently high grades, but surely there had to be another way to help with that. Drugs couldn't possibly be the only answer.

I told his teacher that tests only showed what he cared to let her see on any given day. If he felt she liked him, he would show her more. But if he felt her apathy, he wouldn't care what she saw in him and he would not perform well on a test. It had more to do with their relationship than his intelligence; I truly believed that. And I also believed that was a credit to him and his ability to observe others. My boy was incredibly intelligent, and he wasn't going to jump through hoops for someone who had already written him off. This woman just didn't care to see that.

Still, we agreed to take Brendan to the pediatrician for an ADHD evaluation. He gave us a checklist and another for the teacher—the one who already didn't like him. From this, he determined, yes indeed, Brendan had ADHD. He handed me a prescription for Ritalin and sent us on our way.

This did not convince me. I knew doctors were diagnosing ADHD in record numbers, almost always with boys. I also knew some things that most parents didn't, including the fact that ADHD and RAD (Reactive Attachment Disorder) share many of the same symptoms.

I returned once more to Dr. Fuller's office, where he explained how to tell the difference:

"Let's say you work in the county jail and a man is brought in late at night. He's obviously drunk and he thinks he's Jesus. How do you know if the man is just drunk or also psychotic and delusional? You sober him up and see how he acts in the morning. If he wakes up and asks what he did the night before and how he got there, and seems like a man waking up with a hangover, you have a drunken man on your hands. If, however, he still believes he's Jesus, you have a drunk man who's sobering up, but also needs to be tested for some kind of mental illness."

"So how do I know if my son has ADHD or RAD?" I questioned. To which he replied, "You do attachment therapy to heal the RAD and, when that is done, you see what's left. If there are still symptoms of ADHD, treat them, but they will probably be greatly reduced by that point."

So through the fall of 2000, we did just that. We worked on attachment therapy with Brendan, hoping to treat the root cause of the issue rather than a single symptom. We also saw an "educational diagnostician," who specialized in treating kids without medication. She helped Brendan learn to focus and teach both sides of his brain to work together better. With the combination of these treatments, Brendan's behavior began to improve incrementally. More importantly to me, however, he attached and bonded with us stronger than he ever had.

Slowly at first—and sometimes in fits and bursts—over the next few years our son began to realize once more that *we* were the ones he *could* rely upon and trust.

If only it would be that easy with our next child...

Chapter Twelve

*A*FTER SEVERAL VISITS with Dr. Fuller, we knew we needed to try therapeutic holding[1] with Brendan. Dr. Fuller explained this procedure thoroughly before we tried it.

On Katie's eighth birthday, Brendan woke up detached and in a nasty mood. He refused to find his homework, eat breakfast, or talk about what bothered him. I knew if I sent him to school, the teachers would have to deal with his poor behavior. So instead, I took this as an opportunity to try the methods we had been discussing and practicing with Dr. Fuller. I kissed Katie goodbye, sang her a quick "Happy Birthday," and sent her off to school.

I told Brendan we were going to try out the fun exercise we had learned from Dr. Fuller. He called it a "burrito roll." I got a lightweight sheet and put it on the floor. Brendan excitedly lay down and let me roll him up. Because of Brendan's size, and to protect us both, I wrapped his arms tightly, like a swaddled newborn baby. I made sure to keep his face uncovered so he could breathe easily, before I started.

I picked him up and held him across my lap, like when he was swaddled in a blanket as an infant, with his face against my cheek. I stroked his cheek and told him how much I loved him. He liked it…for about 20 seconds. In

---

1 Holding therapy is no longer a prescribed course of treatment. Since Reactive Attachment Disorder (RAD) is a fairly new diagnosis, please seek out the newest, most proven treatment for your children. Do not attempt holding therapy without the guidance of a trained specialist.

our training, Dr. Fuller had warned us that he would enjoy this exercise until he felt out of control. He had described the process for us, and our experience followed his prediction exactly.

First, Brendan said, "Okay, Mom, that's enough." His words got louder, faster, and more urgent. Within two minutes he started screaming and thrashing to get away. Kids with attachment issues *need* love and parenting, but don't *want* it. They want to be left alone, so they can control their world. I intended to show him my love whether he wanted it or not, simply because he needed it, and even though I knew that he would object.

For parents who have never dealt with an attachment-challenged child, this may seem uncomfortable or extreme, or even abusive. The truth is, for most children, you *wouldn't* violate their boundaries in such a way. You wouldn't push yourself on them when they say "no," and you wouldn't force physical contact and affection when they have clearly voiced their discontent. But the problem is that for children suffering from RAD, they will always voice that discontent. And the only way to push past this and help to almost "reset" their connection pathways is to ignore their objections and to show them that you are going to continue loving and protecting them, no matter what—whether they like it or not.

I won't pretend that it is easy or natural, because it isn't, but…if your child's ability to love and connect with other human beings for the rest of their lives was relying on your ability to step outside your own comfort zone in that moment, you might be surprised at what you would be willing to do.

My mom helped me with the first holding, talking me through the steps and keeping me calm, even as Brendan's own levels of anger and anxiety flew through the roof. I never raised my voice or said anything cruel. I only spoke lovingly and touched him in ways that would feel good to a securely attached child. I touched his face, arms, back. I whispered in his ear and kissed him. On most days, he accepted this affection like any other child, but when he felt unattached, he turned away from it.

His objections turned physical now, as he thrashed his head into my chest, neck, and face. I thought he broke my nose at one point. He spit in my face several times, and, as I had been warned, used the worst language he knew at eight years of age: He called me "stupid head" again and again. I actually chuckled and felt so thankful that he couldn't come up with anything worse.

After exhausting his body from the thrashing, he stopped moving and stared straight ahead. I sensed him gathering strength for round two. After several minutes, the words started again, then the thrashing. Next came the threats. He told me he needed to go to the bathroom. Since our training foretold of this effort to escape, I had made sure he had already gone. I told him to go right there if he had to. He didn't.

Next, he threatened to call Bob. Then the police. I ignored all of this, keeping at it for two and a half hours, until he finally gave up. He sank into my arms and snuggled his head next to my cheek. We lay there until he regained his strength and cuddled closer. Then the words started: "I love you, Mom. Hey, want to watch TV and cuddle? I love you, Mom."

Growing up in the church, I had always been told that God could handle our anger. It is better to bring our hurt feelings and rage to him than to turn away from him in times of frustration. God loves us no matter what angry words we threw—just as a parent always loves their child.

I thought about how God loves us as my little boy cuddled against me and the love I felt for him came rushing through our bond. He had needed to get out his hatred, anger, and rage in a safe way. He knew I could take it, so this experience enabled him to release it. When he released it, he could accept love and give love in return once more. He clung by my side the rest of that day. I held Brendan like this more than 50 times throughout his adolescence, and every time, our bond was only strengthened. He could feel the difference after I held him. Even though he felt the loss of control at the beginning, the payoff was worth it to him, so he continued to let me hold him.

I talked to family and friends about our therapy and how it worked. One relative was the most vocal against this therapy option, telling me he thought it was cruel to restrain our children against their will. Brendan knew we were speaking on the phone one night, and he heard what our conversation was about. He asked if he could explain to the relative what it felt like for him.

With his 10-year-old wisdom, he said, "I feel like I'm out of control and it scares me. My mom holds me and I hate it. I don't want her to hold me, but I know I need it. I can't get back in control on my own. I fight her for a while, but then I give in and feel safe again. After that, I don't want to go away from my mom, and I am happy."

He didn't question my parenting again.

As Brendan got bigger, we transitioned from holding to what Dr. Fuller called, "holding, without holding." When Brendan started to become argumentative or belligerent, I pulled him in close. Usually, this meant sitting very close together on the couch. We'd sit together as I rubbed his back, or played with his hair. If he seemed to accept the touch, I'd let him move a little farther away, but still in the same room. As he regained his positive attitude, he had freedom to move to a different room, or go outside. If the poor behavior returned, I pulled him close again.

I wondered if Katie's time under the lights after her birth might have caused her to have attachment issues as well. The subject was so often on my mind around this time, it was possible I saw attachment issues in even normal behavior. I decided to hold her to see how she reacted. She had seen me hold Brendan, and I asked if she would like to let me hold her in the same way. Katie loved to try anything new, and I even think she may have been experiencing a bit of jealousy over the extra affection Brendan was getting, so without hesitation she replied that yes, she wanted to try. I wrapped her up like a burrito and got down next to her. We cuddled together for about an hour talking, as I stroked her hair and face. She loved it. I asked if anything bothered her, and she replied, "Well, your breath stinks, but that's about it."

It was then that I knew Katie had attached just fine.

Chapter Thirteen

I WILL NEVER FORGET one summer vacation to South Carolina, when Brendan began complaining about his brown eyes. He wanted blue eyes like Bob, Katie, and me; he wanted to look like the rest of his family.

We had never hidden the details of his adoption from him, and he knew and understood where he came from. But he still went through phases of wishing he looked more like the rest of us. By now, I had been doing enough research on adoption to understand the scars that remain, and so I ached for my boy and this expression of grief even he didn't fully comprehend.

As we walked along the boardwalk near the ocean, his current plight had already been on my mind when we came across a Ben and Jerry's ice cream store. Outside, the sign read, "Free sprinkles for anyone with brown eyes!" Brendan proudly went to the counter to receive his free sprinkles. The rest of us enjoyed our un-sprinkled cones.

I felt God's presence as I watched my son eat his ice cream with a twinkle in his beautiful brown eyes. And I allowed myself to believe that everything was going to be just fine.

Our first experience with the adoption agency had been wonderful. During Brendan's adoption, they genuinely seemed to care about all three of us in the adoption triad (birth mother, child, and adoptive parents), doing whatever they could to protect and guide us all equally. Even though we went through the same agency, our second experience felt different. We got the impression that the priority was now about placing children in homes, not necessarily ensuring those homes were prepared to take them. We knew they really cared about orphans, but we had so many questions, and couldn't help but feel as though the agency's level of concern for adoptive parents was nowhere near as high as it had once been.

Our hearts went out to the children. That was why we wanted to adopt in the first place, but without support for us as well, the children could not be served. Bob and I had many frustrating conversations that began with questions and ended with the agency personnel frustrated with us for having so many questions. We wanted to be good parents, so we didn't understand why our questions frustrated them so much. Wasn't that their job?

What can you tell us about the orphanage?

How do they treat them more like family, so that the risk of attachment issues is lowered?

Can we have him checked out by a doctor before we agree to the adoption?

What if we get to Vietnam and find his condition is worse than we had been told?

What if he obviously doesn't like us, and doesn't want to come with us? While we are there, could we be matched with a child who might fit in better with our family?

At the training sessions we attended, comments were made about wealthy white Americans wanting to adopt. In the agency's opinion, these people treated adoption with a consumer mentality. The agency workers felt their mission was to place children in homes. They didn't like bossy people who treated them like they were performing a service, like waiters in a restaurant. We understood their thinking, but we were on the other side of this relationship. It didn't feel good to be told that we were selfish and bossy, simply because we had questions and concerns.

At one point, they told us that this adoption had to take priority over everything else in our lives and that we needed to be ready and willing to put everything on hold or let anything go that might get in the way. That wasn't a possibility though. We already had two children. Brendan and Katie were just as important to us as our new child.

A perfect example of this was a family trip I had earned through my company to Disney World. Brendan and Katie had assisted me with various aspects of my job for a year and a half to help earn this trip. *They* had earned it just as much as I had. Before we ever even started the adoption process, we had promised them the trip to Disney World.

I asked the agency if we could talk about travel dates in order to ensure all our schedules matched up, but instead of going over possibilities with me, they said that if I wasn't willing to totally drop everything else, then maybe we shouldn't adopt. That seemed crazy to me.

Pampered Chef scheduled the Disney trip for the first week in December. I tried to see how we could work the travel plans in with our two required trips to Vietnam. At one point I thought it would be great to be able to take our new son with us to Disney World. In retrospect, I am eternally grateful that did not work out—he would have been unbelievably overwhelmed at the time.

As I tried to get some travel dates to confirm our Vietnam trips as well as the Disney trip, the agency workers got frustrated with me. They didn't know when we would be traveling, but they wouldn't explain the process to me. I could tell they thought I was one of those "consumer" parents just wanting to order up their child and have him delivered to their front door. I didn't even know how to dispel their inaccurate assumptions and I was growing more and more frustrated on my end too.

But by this point, if we wanted our son, we had to stay with this agency. We had to find a way to make it work. And I did want it to work, desperately, for *all* of my children. If we needed to let the Disney trip go, fine. I just wanted to be in the loop.

In the middle of all this frustration, I woke up one morning with the flu. My temperature was high and all I wanted to do was sleep, which is exactly what I was doing when the phone woke me. I only answered because I saw the agency's number on the caller ID, and they were normally so hard to reach. As I picked up the phone, I could hardly talk and I felt horrible with aches and pains.

The social worker on the other end of the line told me that all of the workers at the agency were sick of my questions, and I needed to stop calling them. I sat up in bed stunned. I was already feeling terribly ill and this just pushed me over the edge. I started sobbing on the phone.

I have always been quick to tears, so I wasn't totally surprised by my own reaction, but I guess it caught her off guard. She hung up and immediately called my husband at work. To Bob, she questioned my stability and asked his opinion. She wondered if my emotional health could carry me through this adoption.

Since that time, I have wondered about this. If she had those concerns, shouldn't she have brought them to my attention, or suggested I see a psychologist? Her job required her to make sure the child she placed went to a stable home. Why didn't she follow through on that? If she really had a concern, her job demanded that she address it.

She called to discuss the matter with Bob. He knew me, and understood my concerns about the trip dates. He also knew that when I felt sick, I cried. He wasn't concerned about my mental health, but it didn't feel very good to have it questioned this far into the process.

In the end, all of our travels worked as we hoped, and we were able to squeeze everything in—including the two separate trips to Vietnam required by Vietnamese law in response to recent baby selling scams.

We went as a family to Ho Chi Minh City to meet our son right before Thanksgiving.

It was a trip that would change all of our lives forever.

Chapter Fourteen

*F*OUR EXCITED, NERVOUS travelers boarded a plane from Denver to L.A. two hours late on November 10, 2000 to meet the newest member of the O'Toole family—Sam. We gave him a short name, easy to pronounce and spell. The first flight passed quickly, then we took off from L.A. to Taipei, Taiwan, at midnight.

Brendan and Katie couldn't sleep due to excitement over the jumbo jet ride and getting to meet their new brother. The flight attendants prepared fresh Cup 'O Noodles each time the kids asked, so they loaded up. They also loved the slippers provided on the plane.

We finally arrived in Ho Chi Minh City in the afternoon, emerging from the airport to massive crowds. Swarms of people held up signs, screamed, waved, and crowded around arriving passengers. The chaos unnerved us.

Before too long, we spotted a sign with our name on it—our guide awaiting our arrival. The trip from the airport to the hotel created a whole different kind of adventure. We saw and smelled things we had never experienced before. The sheer number of people stunned us all into silence. Our faces plastered the windows of the van as we drove. We saw a family of five on a single scooter, people selling soup on the sidewalk, others squatting almost to the ground but without a chair as they ate. Our noses were accosted with the smells of garbage, sour milk, urine, and oppression.

We checked in to the Dragon Hotel and tried to get some sleep. We had such an exciting day ahead though that none of us slept well. At 3:00

in the morning, both kids were up and bouncing on the strange little beds, chatting excitedly about going to meet their brother.

The time arrived to leave for the orphanage. Our guide told us to call him "Uncle No Problem," because if we listened to him, we "would have no problem." We usually called him "Uncle." We never fully learned his Vietnamese name, but it sounded something like *Yaum*.

We really liked him. He clearly cared deeply for these children, and they loved him. We boarded a van with four other couples to go meet our new children together.

The ride took about an hour and gave us a chance to see Saigon. I could not figure out how the traffic worked. The crowded city streets consisted mostly of mopeds and bicycles, followed by huge trucks, and then a few cars. The light turned red and everyone pulled up as close to the front of the line as they could. Scooters all scurried in close together at the front. Everyone just seemed to sense when it was time for the other traffic to have his or her turn. They stopped together and started together, even though only the main streets had stoplights.

Many people wore masks for protection from the pollution. Women sometimes wore long gloves to protect their skin from the sun. Unlike in the U.S., women believed lighter skin was beautiful, so they avoided the sun at all costs. Many women wore the customary Aio Dia—long sleeved silk outfits with slits up the sides, and long silk pants underneath. They wore these beautiful garments as they rode bicycles and scooters through the streets.

School children walked in uniforms, businessmen rode scooters, and storefront shops bustled. We heard honking and traffic noises reminiscent of New York City, only louder.

We arrived at the orphanage not knowing what to expect. The Vietnamese people seemed confident that they knew what they were doing, but they didn't share their plans with us. They put all of the adoptive families in a room and told us to wait. Shortly afterward, they brought babies in to the families awaiting infants.

They finally came in with a little three-and-a-half year-old boy— *our* little boy. His nerves showed as he kept a few fingers in his mouth throughout the introductions. Since he didn't understand any English, they told him to call me "Ma" and Bob "Ba." Brendan and Katie's names didn't change. We realized that to this little orphan, Ma and Ba were just words. He didn't know the makeup or ranking of a family.

He had known only this orphanage since his birthmother delivered him in a hospital. She had checked in under a false name and left before the doctor released her. The orphanage workers picked him up at five days old. This had been his home and the only family he'd ever known. They tried to make him hug us, and he hesitantly moved forward.

I could only imagine how confused and scared he must have been. This didn't resemble the movie *Annie*, where orphans couldn't wait to be adopted, as they hoped and dreamed for a family. He seemed content with his home, and didn't understand who we were.

We came to see that the adults didn't regard the children highly, so they didn't bother trying to explain things to them. The kids just went along with whatever happened and learned not to ask questions. We presented Sam, whose Vietnamese name was Binh Quang, with a box of Ritz Crackers. He opened them quickly to share with all the kids back in the room in which he lived, not seeming to care that we followed closely behind.

This was our first look into his life.

Fifteen to twenty beds lined both of the long walls in this room. Turquoise in color, they were about the size of a toddler bed, but with bars like a crib. Children slept on reed mats instead of mattresses. We later learned this made them easier to clean when the children wet the beds. They just hosed them off and used them again.

We tried to use Sam's Vietnamese name at this point, because he didn't yet know the name *Sam*. I don't think we pronounced it very well though, and most of the time he ignored us when we called him.

The children all seemed to know the universal language of play, and Brendan and Katie quickly found their way alongside the other children. The agency had suggested we leave them home on this first trip, giving Sam the opportunity to bond with Bob and me. But we thought the kids might make it easier for him, due to his age. We were right. The three of them started playing almost immediately. Curtains in the window made for a great game of peek-a-boo with Katie. He laughed adorably for the first time since our arrival.

We had collected a huge suitcase full of small toy donations for the orphanage and we gave them to the workers. We wanted to make sure there were enough for all the children, so this bag was stuffed. Once we handed them off, however, we never saw those toys being played with by any of the children. We wondered if the money they made selling those toys was actually how they fed the kids, and was therefore infinitely more important.

Other than the beds, a TV monitor hung from the high ceiling, the only object in the room. As we entered the room, several kids sat on the floor straining their necks to watch Disney's *Beauty and the Beast* dubbed in Vietnamese.

Uncle brought our family water bottles to help with the 100-degree temperatures and high humidity. He gave water to Sam as well. Sam went to all the other children, offering them a drink from his water, and some of his crackers. We could see immediately that he had a kind and giving heart. He seemed to enjoy being one of the older kids, giving instructions to the younger ones around him and acting in the role of a leader.

Scott, a friend we had met through our state-mandated classes, later told us his impression of Sam when he had watched him on his first trip to see his own children. Apparently Sam had stood against a post with his arms crossed, telling the other children what to do. Scott said he looked like the "kingpin" of the three- and four-year-olds.

We played with the children for a few hours, trying to give attention to all of the kids. We attempted to hug and hold as many as we could. They seemed starved for attention. The women caregivers all appeared kind and gentle, but it became clear that they were totally outnumbered.

There could never be enough time in the day for them to give any meaningful attention to even a few of these children. They fed them and made sure they had clothing. They cleaned the facility as best they could, but the care these kids received did not extend beyond that. There just weren't enough hands.

None of the boys wore underwear. We realized that clothes were community property. Each day, they wore whatever they were given. Most of the clothing had lettering from the United States, so we thought it had likely all been donated and well worn. These kids were not filthy, but they played on a dirt playground and never took baths or showers. They had only sponge baths, meaning there was still some pretty old dirt living on these little ones.

The playground included a metal slide and two small rickety swing sets. Other than that, they played with the dirt or made up games.

On our brief tour, we saw a few classrooms and it appeared that they tried to teach the younger children to write with paper and pencils. The older children went to public school very early in the morning and returned around noon. Their afternoons were spent feeding the babies, doing laundry by hand, cooking, cleaning, and completing their homework.

Scott's family was planning to adopt twin girls. His family had met the girls on their first trip to Vietnam, and was waiting the required six weeks to return and take them home. We promised to look in on them, just as they had looked in on Sam for us. For some reason, the caretakers had put them in a room with the children who had Hepatitis C, quarantining them. They didn't have Hepatitis C. We asked to see them, but the workers hesitated. We explained that we knew their parents and wanted to take back pictures of how well treated the twins were. Only then did they let us see the girls.

I was speechless when we first saw the twins. They were about nine months old and could barely lift their heads to look at us. I picked them up one at a time and tried to gently touch them all over. I spoke softly to them. They seemed to respond after a few minutes by meeting my eyes. They were totally neglected and I could see they were failing to thrive. These girls needed to be home, with their parents, as soon as possible.

Another little girl we knew would also be going home soon was staying in Sam's room. She had a sad, empty look on her face. All of the kids had some scabies, but she had the worst case as far as I could tell. A bacterium that burrows under the skin, these rashes are itchy and painful and this poor little girl was covered in it.

As we walked through the orphanage, we noticed they segregated the children. Some were divided by age grouping, others by disease or disability.

The sick children were kept from the well children, but, as we saw with the twins, this method didn't always work out the way they intended.

In one room, we saw a girl of about 14 or 15 scooting around on the floor. Her physical deformity caught us off guard, and I fought to divert my eyes. But it was the next stop that truly ate away at me. Our collective breath released as we entered the infant room.

It held more than 50 cribs.

There were so many babies, two per crib and lined up sideways next to each other. The silence really disturbed us. There were approximately one hundred babies in that room, aged newborn to six months, and we didn't hear a sound. None of them cried. They had learned early on that crying did not bring them what they needed, so they didn't even try anymore. I picked up and stroked as many babies as I could in the short time we were there.

My heart broke as I pictured Sam, once a newborn in this same room.

Chapter Fifteen

As we walked the grounds of the orphanage, I watched Brendan reach out to hold his new little brother's hand. Sam shook his hand free, stepping a foot or two away without acknowledgement. I saw the dejected face of my little boy, knowing he had just been trying to bond with his brother. This sweet eight-year-old who had taken a leap and reached for a child's hand did not understand why that affection had been rebuffed. From then on, the boys never really connected.

Uncle told us we needed to head back to the hotel. The orphanage couldn't feed us and they needed to serve the children lunch. Without informing us of his plans, Uncle asked Sam if he would like to go with us. Sam jumped in the van. I did some math in my head. We had been there for several hours already, and Sam had not used a toilet. The van ride home would take at least an hour. We needed a bathroom break before we could leave.

Uncle showed me the way to the restroom, and told me to take Sam with me. This poor little boy. Obviously he had never used a toilet in his life. He started to go on the floor, so I slowly inched him towards the ceramic seat he seemed so unsure of. He screamed in protest, so I let him go on the floor. I told Uncle about it and said only that he wouldn't be allowed to do that in the hotel. Uncle laughed and told me to ask the front desk for a bucket. This seemed totally normal for him.

Welcome to a Vietnamese orphanage, I thought.

I would not allow him to go in a bucket at the hotel, so I told Brendan that his first job as Sam's big brother would be to show him how to use the potty. What a great job for an eight-year-old boy! Brendan loved his task and performed it well.

The drive back to the hotel became much more lively than the drive there earlier that morning. Sam had never been in a car, and there were no seat belts. He jumped and laughed and screamed, acting a bit crazy and as though he was hyped up on sugar. At first it seemed really funny and we all cracked up with laughter. After he didn't calm down though, we started to get a little worried. This didn't appear to be normal child behavior. But then again, what was normal?

Everyone needed to eat when we returned to the hotel. Uncle dropped us off, so we fended for ourselves. We decided it might be best to stay put and get used to each other before trying to venture out of the hotel. We called room service, but couldn't read the menu, so we ordered four plates of different items.

When the food arrived, we gave each person a plate and a fork. Brendan and Katie started putting a little of every item on their plates to sit down and eat. Sam loved his new freedom and the excitement it brought, so much so that he didn't seem capable of slowing down. We watched in horror as our new son grabbed food off plates, stuffed his mouth over and over, and ran around the room laughing until he threw up.

Bob and I didn't eat a thing. I felt sick to my stomach. Rather than a young child, Sam looked more like a wild animal that had been let out of a cage, totally out of control, and laughing with a fiendish cackle.

What were we doing? What had we gotten ourselves into? Only one hour had passed with our new son, and he seemed absolutely crazy.

"Good thing these are baby teeth!" I told Bob as we got a closer look at Sam's mouth. So many teeth were cracked, missing, or broken. I mentally made a list of doctors we would need to visit soon after arriving home: dentist, pediatrician, and what other doctors might we need?

Most memories from the rest of that day escape me. We went to an outdoor market to buy clothes, because they sent Sam with us in shorts, a shirt, and horrible thick, leather boots without socks, but no personal belongings or extra clothing. He had a scar up the back of his ankle and his left foot looked unusual.

We bought underwear, even though the clerk thought we were silly to make him wear "two pants."

Bedtime couldn't come quickly enough. Brendan and Katie fell asleep as soon as their heads hit the pillow. Sam, on the other hand, grew very agitated. He didn't know this hotel, or who we were. No one had told him anything. They had just dumped him off at this unknown location with strangers, and hadn't told him if or when he would be going back to the only home he had ever known. He appeared terrified.

We did our best to soothe him, but sleep came fitfully for Sam. He didn't like the air-conditioned room, so I paced the balcony with him in my arms, exposing him to the familiar feel of humidity and the sounds of the busy city. I carried my 35-pound son for almost two hours until his body couldn't stay awake another minute. His lack of trust showed in his fight to stay alert. I had to make sure to continue walking for several minutes after he fell asleep, because any change in movement caused him to jolt back awake.

Sam stayed with us for five days. During that time, we observed a boy with no self-regulation, no fear, and no ability to feel pain. He ran head-first into a brick wall, which propelled him backwards onto a cement floor. We heard his head crack onto the floor, but instead of crying, he lay there, laughing hysterically.

He would not stay seated at restaurants and he volleyed back and forth between hyperactivity and zombie-like withdrawal. Everywhere we went he followed along in a sort of trance. He didn't seem to care what we did or where we went. He didn't appear carefree or happy, as we had been told by the adoption agency—just resigned to go through the motions and survive moment to moment.

Before arriving in Vietnam, people had warned us about the police. They had told us to avoid them at all costs because they didn't like Americans.

When we visited the zoo, four AK-47 wielding soldiers stopped us and asked if the three kids belonged to us. Bob and I glanced at each other. We nodded that they did. One of the soldiers pulled out a camera and asked us to take a picture of them with our children. We agreed, and quickly found our own camera to document this moment. They were friendly and curious, not rude or angry.

Many of Sam's conditions were much more severe than we had been told. Concerns crept into our conversations when the kids were out of earshot. We called our liaison back in Denver to discuss our apprehension. We addressed the issues and said we wanted to make sure this was a good fit for him and for our family before plucking him away from everything he knew. "What if his problems are too much for us to handle?" we asked with a shamed hesitation.

Suddenly, we couldn't believe we were even questioning this decision. Before we had arrived in Vietnam, we had been so sure! Sam was our son. We knew that. It was just frightening to be looking at this boy and realizing we had been lied to about his condition. It was frightening to watch *our son* behaving like a wild animal. Parental instincts kicked in, and more than anything, we simply wanted to know that he was okay. And if he wasn't, we wanted to know how we could help.

Brendan and Katie were already calling Sam their brother and couldn't wait to take him home. We didn't know what to do, as we were so conflicted with a roller coaster of emotions. Every minute felt like it resulted in a swing of the pendulum. We called our liaison during one of those down moments, crying as we told her our concerns. She harshly told us that if we didn't want him, we needed to take him back to the orphanage and go home. We asked about an option of selecting a child with fewer problems—not wanting to treat this adoption like picking a puppy up from the pound, but also not feeling like this was what we had signed up for. She reminded us that they had chosen *this* child for us. If we wanted another child, we needed to take him back, go home, and start the process all over again.

It felt like she was trying to strong-arm us into a decision, but this time we held firm with our concerns. The report provided by the agency had listed him as a happy, well-adjusted child with Hepatitis B. Now that we were with him, we realized the report had inaccurately described so much, and we needed to know the truth before we made a final decision.

She set up an appointment for me to take him to a western medical clinic for an evaluation.

The next day, we went to the clinic looking for answers. Bob stayed with Brendan and Katie while I packed our youngest up to go. My mind was swirling in a thousand different directions. I felt like I had entered The Twilight Zone. I held the hand of my broken little Vietnamese boy as we met the French doctor. "Mademoiselle" he regarded me. When a nurse bribed Sam to stand on the scale with a piece of candy, I realized that I at least now understood how his teeth had gotten so bad.

The doctor assured me that his hearing was probably normal. "You don't pronounce his name correctly, and the kids have 'selective listening' because the orphanage is so loud. He'll be fine as soon as you get him home and it's quiet." He also told me there was nothing to be concerned about with the scabies, the foot, the teeth, the pain tolerance, or his lack of words. All of these things could be dealt with in the United States, he explained.

Bob and I decided we would do whatever it took to bring him back to health. We would love this little boy with everything we had. If God had chosen him for us, God would take care of making it work.

With that settled, we visited the orphanage one last day before heading back to the States. In hindsight, this was a bad idea. Sam must have thought he was going back for good. He stayed with the other children for lunch while they showed us more of the orphanage. When he saw us after lunch, he began pushing other children wildly on the swing, almost with the intention of hurting them, and seemingly in rebellion. The spiteful look in his eyes sent chills down my spine.

Again, fear crept in. It was his laughter at pain, his unwillingness (or inability) to listen or follow our commands, and his out of control behavior that scared us. What if we were going to damage our family by bringing this child home with us? What if his needs were greater than we could actually handle?

But then again, how could we possibly go home without him? The nuns had chosen this child for *us*. When a family requested to adopt a child, the nuns would pray together for a unanimous decision they felt came from God. If God had chosen Sam for us, shouldn't we trust in that choice?

After all, we had heard our entire lives that God never gives people more than they can handle...

Chapter Sixteen

WE HAD SOME interesting cultural experiences that week, amidst the stress and concern for our son. We visited a market called "The Chinese Market." Cambodian refugee children went there to beg for money and food. I remember wondering how bad Cambodia must be, if the children saw this as an improved environment for begging.

Filth covered their bodies, since they lived on the streets and could not bathe. Their out-stretched hands greeted us each time our car stopped, and they followed us everywhere we went. Uncle had warned us about this before we arrived, so we felt somewhat prepared. He told us we stood out because of our skin, hair, and height. Everyone in the market watched us. These children were professional beggars, with big, sad eyes and pouty lips that tugged at our heartstrings. But we had been warned that if we gave money to any of them, it could literally start a riot. The sight broke our hearts. These were the poorest children we had ever seen and we knew our money could help many.

Uncle made sure to give one child in the group some money after we were all back in the car, only as he was closing his door to drive off. He explained they would share, but it wouldn't cause anyone to get hurt by doing it that way.

At the same market, a poor Vietnamese woman saw us with Sam. She knew instantly that we would be giving him a home in America. She approached us with her baby and made movements of putting food into the baby's mouth. This baby needed food, and her mother wanted us to take her. If the law had allowed it, I would have adopted that baby also, on the spot. How desperate must a mother feel to cause her to try to give her child to a complete stranger? She knew we could afford to take care of her baby and she couldn't—more heartbreak.

Katie's long blond hair especially stood out in the crowd. The Vietnamese women loved it, and dragged Katie away from Bob and me to show their friends. They wanted to touch her hair. This scared Katie, even though she never left our sight. We told her, "It's OK, sweetie, they just like your hair." They did not have the same regard for personal space as Americans.

Each morning, the hotel restaurant had a small selection to choose from: omelets, French bread with jam, or Pho, which is a hot soup served with chicken or beef. The first morning, the waiter asked Sam what he wanted, and Sam bowed when the waiter mentioned Pho with beef. It occurred to us that he had never eaten meat, because he ate the soup, but didn't touch the beef. The rest of us typically had an omelet or French bread. By the end of our stay, we had grown very weary of our options.

During our time at the Dragon Hotel, we observed men urinating on the outside of buildings and on trees. They did not appear to be homeless men, and this practice didn't seem to offend the locals.

One afternoon, I stayed with Sam for a nap, while Bob took Brendan and Katie out. When he woke up, we walked around outside the hotel.

A commotion caught our attention, so we went across the block to see about the gathering. A man on a bicycle had a six-foot snake in his basket. The man cut into the snake and put the venom in small plastic containers and sold them to the people in the crowd. They believed the venom had healing powers, and paid large amounts of money for it.

Exchanging money at the hotel reminded us of our wealth. We needed money to pay for many of the government services with our adoption, and they only took cash. We gave them $100 USD and received $1,000,000 Dong—that's one million. We asked the front desk workers how much money they made and they told us about $30 per month. We exchanged $100 at the desk at least three times over a five-day period. We realized they must think we were rich. I heard people say that if you lived in the United States, you were rich. I finally understood: I was rich.

Early in the week, we ordered handmade silk Aui Dai's, traditional Vietnamese outfits, for each of us. Brendan and Sam picked the same material, so the brothers matched. Katie and I did the same. The workers told us when to return for the clothing. They should have been ready the morning we had to take Sam back to the orphanage, but they were not finished. I felt so disappointed about this. We couldn't communicate with Sam, but I had convinced myself he might realize he belonged to us if he saw Katie and me matching, as well as him and Brendan. There was nothing that could be done, though. They simply weren't finished, and that was that.

The day we had to return Sam to the orphanage, we tried to have someone explain to him that we needed to go back to America, but we would soon return to get him and bring him to our home forever. We asked people at the hotel, people on the street, workers at the orphanage, and anyone else we knew understood English. Each time we were met with the response, "He's just a child. He's fine." No one would explain for us and we couldn't tell him ourselves. Once again, we were unable to help our new son. It seemed completely remiss of the culture to not think that a child needed or deserved an explanation about the details of his life.

On the way to the orphanage, Uncle decided we should have a little fun, so he took us to a dilapidated amusement park. He didn't seem to mind the pouring rain. In the United States, we would call that amount of rain a flood. People rode their bicycles and scooters through the foot or more of rushing water as if it happened everyday. During monsoon season, I suppose it did.

We spent a few hours covered with rain slickers, sloshing through huge amounts of standing water to find rides that were operational. The weather matched our moods.

Our hearts broke as the orphanage staff once again pushed Sam toward each of us and told him to kiss us. This time he kissed each of us on the cheek and we hugged him and said goodbye. We sobbed as they led him away for his lunch.

Katie said, "Oh Mommy, why can't we just take him now? Why do we have to leave him?" How do you explain to a child Vietnamese adoption laws? The waiting period and two-trip requirement was customary, to ensure the true dedication of adoptive parents. But it was difficult for even us to understand, so of course the children were struggling.

The day continued in much the same manner. Uncle took us to a "fancy restaurant" where the mascot, a local dog, pooped on the floor next to our table.

Fitting.

For our last meal in Vietnam, we ventured out to a restaurant some locals had recommended. The place was a bit creepy, with geckos on the walls and ceilings. When the menus arrived, we had a great laugh over one of the food options, Chicken Penis. This entre, spelled out in English, had no description. The kids thought this was funny, gross, and inappropriate. It became a family joke for years.

We returned to pick up the Aui Dai's later that day, but the special meaning seemed lost now that Sam was back at the orphanage.

Our last and possibly scariest adventure happened at the airport before our departure from Ho Chi Minh City. We looked for gate 7 for quite some time. Our family's combined intelligence was fairly high, but we could not find the gate we were meant to depart from. We saw gates 1,2,3,4,5,6 and 8, but no gate 7. The monitors didn't help. They told us to look for gate 7, but not how to find it. After a good 15 minutes of searching, a young, friendly Vietnamese-American woman asked us if we were looking for gate 7. Yes! She took us there. It was in a totally different part of the terminal.

The hour we spent waiting for our flight passed quickly as she told us her story. Born in Vietnam, her father taught at the university. As Saigon started to fall during the war, her parents took her to the dock to get on a boat. They reassured her they would come right behind her, but they did not get on the boat. She found out much later that her dad had been rescued by helicopter from the roof of the university. She became an orphan on that ship.

The boat took her to an island refugee camp. She didn't know the island's location, but she stayed there for months. Every day, she went to the beach to watch for her parents. They never came. She ended up in the United States in the foster care system. She learned English and became a citizen.

She didn't see her parents for years. They finally reunited, but by this time she had grown up and lived a life in the States. Her parents still lived in Saigon. When we met, her work with Kodak allowed her to travel to Vietnam to visit them frequently. They tried to move to California with her, but they couldn't get used to the lack of noise, the huge homes and yards, the personal space, and the culture. They loved Vietnam, and so they stayed.

This woman treated us with such kindness. We knew her life had broken her, but she had somehow put the pieces back together. It felt as though God had placed her in our path, helping us to see what could be true for Sam as well, with enough love and guidance.

We stood with her as they started to board the plane. We sent the kids through with their tickets, and I followed. Bob was behind me when the agent stopped him, claiming he needed to go back through security because something questionable had been found in his luggage. He took Bob's passport and wouldn't return it to him.

Frightened and unsure of how to proceed, our new friend offered to go with Bob and act as his translator while I helped the kids board. She truly must have been an angel. They rushed back through security to the baggage hold and were shown something from a bag that did not belong to us. The woman held a heated exchange with the airport workers. Bob didn't understand any of what happened, but told them the bag didn't belong to him. Our new friend and the workers argued loudly for several minutes.

Brendan, Katie, and I already had our seats and I worried for Bob. *What if the plane left before he got back? Why had they taken his passport?* We couldn't even contact him, and we were frightened.

Our new friend finally convinced the baggage men to let them go, so she and Bob had to run back through security to the gate. They arrived just in time to be seated, just before the plane began to taxi. I asked what had happened and Bob couldn't speak. He motioned for me to be quiet and we took off. It wasn't until we were at cruising altitude that he felt safe telling me about it.

The woman explained to him that the worker knew we were wealthy Americans and they were trying to extort money from us. The baggage handlers had separated him from his family and threatened him by saying they would restrain him if he didn't give them cash. She fought for him and told the men he wouldn't pay and she would report them. If she hadn't shown up when we were looking for our gate, Bob probably would have missed our flight.

Maybe even worse.

Chapter Eighteen

*W*E ARRIVED HOME just a week after leaving, now feeling as though we were a family member short, with our youngest still what seemed like a million miles away. At this point in our lives, both of our extended families lived nearby and we split holidays between the two. This Thanksgiving Day didn't feel the same as those in the past though. The extravagant amount of food now disgusted us.

In Saigon, we had witnessed families working not from paycheck to paycheck, but from meal to meal. If they had money from sales in the morning, they could eat lunch out on the street. It now felt gluttonous to have so much food before us—food we knew could have fed some of those families for weeks.

All four of us noticed this strange feeling of culture shock in returning to our own hometown. We felt sick to our stomachs and had a difficult time eating or enjoying the day. Our son remained in that place. No one really understood how we felt. How could they? We wanted to talk about our experiences, but most everyone wanted Thanksgiving to be as usual, with football, food, and jovial small talk.

A change took place inside of us. After what we had seen and experienced, small talk didn't fulfill us anymore. We loved these people, but they didn't understand us.

I kept picturing the children scratching their scabies laden skin. Our pediatrician suggested I contact the manufacturer of the medication used to treat the disease. They agreed to donate a case of medication to the orphanage, but I still had to find a translator to make sure the directions were clearly marked in Vietnamese. It felt like such a small thing to do, and I hoped it would bring comfort and relief to many children.

In early December, we took our long-awaited trip to Disney World, but the discomfort remained for Bob and me. We tried to enjoy the Character Breakfasts, free visits to all the parks, special closed events for Pampered Chef trip earners, luxury hotels, and great food. Everyone treated us with kindness. But it all suddenly felt so over-the-top. Disney World could cause culture shock just coming from Denver, but having returned from Saigon, it felt more extreme.

We enjoyed our time as a family, but I couldn't get the sights, sounds, and smells from Vietnam out of my mind. I never forgot that my son still lived in those conditions, and the time couldn't pass quickly enough. For all my fear and apprehension, I now yearned to have him with me—desperate to be able to protect and care for him myself. For the kids' sake, I tried to stay engaged and enjoy the trip, but I really just wanted it to be over so that I could go get Sam out of that place and bring him home.

Finally, six weeks after our initial trip, I was permitted to return for Sam. My mom and my brother, Dave, joined me on that second trip. We couldn't afford to take the kids again, and Bob needed to get back to work, so he stayed home with them.

My mom had provided such support to me when the idea of adopting first came up, and I had approached my brother about joining us early on, thinking he might like to explore his home country. His adoption had occurred at 14 months of age, and he had not been back since. At first he seemed to struggle with the idea of coming with us, but eventually he came around and decided he wanted to join. We left two days before Christmas, following the nighttime sky through our entire 40-hour trip. We totally missed Christmas Eve, but enjoyed some of my mom's cranberry nut bread in Singapore, on what would have been Christmas Eve back home.

We showered in Singapore's airport, and Mom and I changed into dresses. We learned on our first trip that women wear dresses in government offices, and this trip would involve that kind of visit. None of us had slept much on any of our flights, but we felt certain we would have some time to rest when we landed. We had been told that, even in Vietnam, government offices would be closed for Christmas.

Our flight landed in Ho Chi Minh City around 11:00 a.m., but my luggage did not arrive with us. We stood at the lost baggage counter for over an hour filling out paperwork about the missing bag. We left the airport with my mom and Dave's luggage, but I felt deflated knowing that my bag, containing everything I had brought for Sam and for myself, had not made it.

On our first trip, I had heard about a hotel used by dignitaries when visiting Saigon. For just a bit more money, we stayed in a very modern, westernized hotel. We drank the water out of the tap and everything worked exactly as it should. We found this somewhat "normal" hotel well worth the money, when everything else seemed so strange.

Uncle was our chaperone once more, and I was grateful for a familiar face. He dropped us off for what we thought would be a good night's rest, but then he told us to be ready in 20 minutes to head back out.

Our destination: the orphanage.

Our emotions jumped all over the place. I couldn't wait to see Sam, but we needed to sleep. We were all exhausted and drained. I thought that perhaps we could play with the kids for a few hours and then sleep, but Uncle had different plans in mind.

We arrived at the orphanage during naptime. Once again I was reminded of how children in Vietnam were treated. It didn't matter that we arrived while the children slept—they woke them up anyway. Why didn't Uncle let us rest for a few hours, so the children could also finish their naps? The question plagued me, but I knew I would probably never get the answer— at least, not an answer that would be satisfactory to me. Because the truth was, children simply were not considered when making plans. A sleepy Sam came to us, and just as before, they told him to kiss us. I couldn't tell if he remembered me or not. I told him I was "Ma," and introduced Grandma and Dave. Did he wonder about Bob? Or Brendan and Katie? I couldn't be sure, and there was no way to explain the situation to him.

I could only imagine what he thought about these new strangers. I was the only connection from that first trip, and I wasn't even positive he remembered me. His behavior indicated nothing.

He looked right through me.

As we spent time with the children, Sam seemed different. I realized that Katie and Brendan had made it much easier for him on that first trip. Kids know how to play with other kids. Without them, we were just a bunch of strange adults he didn't seem too interested in knowing.

Uncle loaded us into the van and took us to Sam's adoption finalization ceremony; our dress change in Singapore turned out to be quite fortunate. A teacher from the orphanage came to sign the papers on behalf of Sam. In November, they had given me documents to bring back in December. I had them, but couldn't find the right one. I started to panic, and the workers treated me like I had done something horribly wrong. They made a big deal about having to print another copy. The adoption agency told us nothing would be open on Christmas anyway. After such a long journey, and missing all of my belongings, I didn't understand how they could be so frustrated. I was doing my very best.

I remembered back to Brendan's adoption finalization. The judge had said he loved adoptions, because they were celebrations, not crimes. We had taken pictures and had a party. Everything about it had been special. This ceremony, on the other hand, took place in a bland government office with a stainless steel desk and officers in uniforms. They obviously did not see this as a celebration, and I clearly annoyed them. Sam fidgeted and fussed. Luckily, it only took about an hour.

From there, we went to another office. Dave kept Sam in the van because government agencies were not considered places for children. The temperature reached into the high 90's, and I worried they would not be able to stay cool. Uncle gave us instructions to sit in the metal chairs and not ask questions. He said they would call our number when they were ready. He warned us that they thought Americans to be impatient, so if we asked any questions about how long it would take, they would move us to the end of the line. We understood.

"Sit on the hard metal chairs, stare at the blank walls, and be quiet."

We did that for over three hours. Every so often, a worker stuck his head into the room.

No line existed.

No one else waited for anything that day, just the Americans.

When they finally came to help us, they took our paper, made a big scene of stamping it with their seal, and presented it to us. We left immediately and hoped our day was finally coming to an end.

Uncle thought we should make one last stop. According to him, now was a perfect time to get Sam his passport photo. My newly legal son was scared to death and had been sitting in a van with a total stranger all day. How he thought this would be a good idea, I will never know. But we didn't feel as though we were in a position to object either.

The look on his face in those pictures was about as sad as any picture I have ever seen. It still breaks my heart to look back on them.

We finally made our way back to the hotel. I found myself hoping they would take Sam back to the orphanage because of the intensity of our exhaustion. I knew if we had some good sleep, we would be better able to handle all the events the next day would bring. But I had forgotten the adoption was now final; he was completely my responsibility.

The minute Uncle left our hotel room, Sam banged on the door and started to cry. He suddenly seemed desperate to be out of this room and away from us. The door had two sets of locks, one on the doorknob, and a bolt, up high. We had to lock the bolt so he couldn't run out after Uncle.

He stood at the door, trying to escape, as he pounded and cried for over an hour. If I went near him, he screamed louder. I couldn't explain anything to him, or make it better in any way.

This poor little boy probably felt as though he had been orphaned from the orphanage.

He finally sat on the couch next to Dave and calmed down. But I couldn't help but wonder what he knew—what he understood to be true. Had he realized what was happening in court that day? Was that the explanation for his reaction now, so different from the first time he had been in a hotel with us? Was there finality that now frightened him?

The next morning, Uncle picked us up at 9 a.m. He took us to Immigration and Naturalization Services (INS) to apply for Sam's visa. We sat again for over an hour. Luckily, this time Uncle came with us. Sam fell asleep on my mom, and Uncle whispered to me that he had never been held like that before.

When it was finally our turn, an American interviewed me and refused to process Sam's file because the orphanage had missed a single stamp. Uncle had to leave us there to go get the stamp, and only then did they grant the visa.

Over the next two days, Sam went through fits of crying and collapsing from exhaustion. He seemed to only want Dave, oddly connecting with my brother in a way I couldn't quite explain. He woke at one point at three in the morning, crying and refusing to have anything to do with me. He sat on the cold floor by himself. When I held my arms out to pick him up, he crossed his arms over his chest and turned his back on me. Dave came out of his room due to the commotion. Sam held his arms out for Dave to pick him up. The two of them began crying together, and we had to guide Dave towards the couch so that they could at least sit. After 10 minutes of this my mom finally asked him what was going on.

"I just know," he said. "I know how he feels." Even though my brother had been adopted at 14 months old, something about this experience brought him back to a time when an unknown family had also taken him in. Being here now, he said he recognized everything, somehow instinctually remembering the smells of this place, the pain and confusion our boy was now facing.

He just knew.

Later that day we had an opportunity to visit the orphanage for the last time. I presented them with the case of scabies medication. They told me they would not use it, because when the next child came, the children would all be re-infected anyway. I felt horrified that they wouldn't even try to provide relief for the children already in their care.

For some reason, they gave us an inside look that we hadn't seen on our previous visits. We arrived at lunchtime and they asked if Sam wanted to eat. Everything happened so quickly, and we wanted to see the inner workings of the orphanage, so we allowed him to be guided away.

We didn't stop to think this might be harmful to Sam.

What if he thought we were leaving him again?

He followed the kids to eat lunch and we went with Uncle to see the rest of the orphanage.

The first room we saw looked like some sort of meeting room. It had a picture of Ho Chi Minh and the communist sickle and hammer. We saw the kitchen next. They had constructed a five-layer rice cooker that made enough rice for 300 children per meal. It was amazing to see how rice kernels and steam could feed so many.

While we went on the tour, Sam played with the other children. I would catch only glimpses of him here and there, but his play seemed harsh. He kicked a child, and pushed others so high on the swing that it scared them. In retrospect, his anxiety must have had him rejecting anyone and everything around him. He didn't want to be here anymore. He no longer knew where he belonged. He must have been so scared.

We had been told originally to plan on two weeks in Vietnam, but all of our paperwork was completed in just four days. We had seen the offices for Singapore Air a few blocks from our hotel, so after that visit at the orphanage, we walked down to see if we could get an earlier flight.

"Tet," was the response we received to our inquiry. Tet, the Vietnamese New Year, started in January. Once the celebration of Tet began, everything apparently shut down for a month. For us, this meant that anyone trying to get in or out of the country flew the week before Tet, and most flights were completely booked. The agent told us she would let us know if anything opened up, but that we shouldn't plan on it.

That night, Sam woke up at long past midnight and wouldn't let me near him. He started wandering around the apartment whimpering. I left the lights off because I didn't want him to think it was time to get up. Mom and Dave got up and we all just sat on the sofa quietly while he wandered around. After about half an hour, he lay down on the tile floor and continued to cry silently.

I lay down on the couch and left room for him, but acted like I didn't care what he did. He finally gave up and moved beside me, falling right to sleep as I wrapped an arm around him. He tossed and kicked in his sleep. It was like he was fighting the devil all night. He woke a few more times and got up to wander, but always came back.

Uncle picked us up at 7:00 a.m. to go the hospital for his medical visa check. There was no way in the world we could have done this without "Uncle No Problem." He was a godsend. He weaved us through different buildings, to the front of the line, and to the right offices, ensuring everything went smoothly.

We then went to have our final INS interview. It took about an hour and Sam started to get upset because he was so exhausted. Finally, we were able to get him back to the hotel so that he could eat and have a nap. I had already learned that he needed to be held in order to fall asleep. His voice was fading, after all the screaming and crying of the previous days. He would start to cuddle with me, and then—almost as if he was remembering he did not trust me—he would suddenly jerk awake. It happened several times a day, his internal struggle over whether or not to allow me to love him.

The aunt and uncle of another adoptive family came to Vietnam so that they could all spend Christmas together. They were missionaries, making Vietnam closer for them to visit than the United States. I mentioned to them that it seemed as though Sam fought with the devil each and every night, explaining how exhausted we all were. They asked if we were Christians. I responded that my parents had baptized me the day of my birth and I had attended church every Sunday of my life. Of course I called myself a Christian.

They asked if I prayed about Sam's fits in the night. This really bothered me. Of course I prayed about it. I felt as though they were coming across as "holier than thou" and it annoyed both my brother and me. Looking back though, I wish I had asked more about this kind of prayer. I didn't know anything about spiritual warfare. I came from a liturgical church with a tradition of praying pre-written prayers. Praying directly what was in my heart and just speaking to God was new to me.

I tried many times during those two weeks to recite the Lord's Prayer, the only prayer I knew. I felt so far from God, and spiritually afraid. I can see now that the enemy of my new son's soul did not want him to leave this communist country to join a church-going family. Satan did not want this child out of his grasp and he worked hard to prevent it. I am amazed at God's wisdom, compassion, power, and might, even in the midst of my ignorance. I did not understand the spiritual workings going on, but God didn't need me to understand. I truly believe he just needed me to be there.

Our days typically started around three or four in the morning when Sam woke up after wetting the bed. Not long after he got his bearings, the screaming would begin. He liked baths, so we filled a few hours throughout the day with four or five separate baths. The zoo stood within walking distance from our hotel, so that became a regular event as well. Sometimes we saw school children in uniforms. Sam stared at them, and I wondered if he wished he could join them. He went along with us wherever we went, but would only rarely engage.

Uncle had many connections, and used his cell phone regularly. When all the adoption appointments were completed, he made arrangements for us to travel to the orphanage that had been Dave's home for the first 14 months of his life.

At 7:00 a.m. the next day, Uncle returned again to pick us up. He took us first to a market a few hours away, one that had snakes, chickens, and anything that could ever be necessary for a meal.

We needed to use a restroom, so Uncle made a deal with a local family. If we would purchase bottles of Coke from them, we could go through their house to the backyard, where they had a squat-pot. This was a unique hole in the ground, with places for users to position their feet on either side. This amenity came without toilet paper.

While at the market, Sam began to run a fever. He was sick. He rejected my attempts to comfort him, but allowed my mom to hold him. We traveled while Sam slept, crossing over 60 bridges and one river, where we drove aboard the ferry. Our trip lasted 13 hours, with 11 passengers in the van.

Once we arrived in Soc Trang, Uncle got on the phone and used Dave's adoption papers to find the director of the orphanage. We walked a few blocks and that director met us and took us on a tour of what used to be the orphanage.

She did not remember Dave, but said that according to the time he had been there, she would have been the one to name him. Her name was Sister Mary Margaret and she was the sweetest little lady. She held Dave's hand and told him she was his first mother.

The orphanage was now a home for poor children. They were not orphans, but their parents couldn't afford to raise them, so they stayed at the home. Some of the children would go back to their parents on weekends, but if they lived too far, they only returned to their family during the summer. The children were so sweet and they sang songs for us.

From there, we went to dinner. Sam acted up at the restaurant, and I felt awkward doing anything about it, because I didn't understand this culture. We needed to stay in a different hotel each night, and Sam had an even more difficult time than normal getting to sleep. I felt awful. He had barely gotten the chance to get used to one hotel, and now we were uprooting him once more. He cried for a long time, but finally fell asleep.

At 7:00 a.m. the next day, the van was ready to leave again. We visited a Cambodian Buddhist temple, ate breakfast, and drove through some of the most backcountry roads I had ever imagined. Everyone just kept repeating, "I can't believe this." We took a boat ride unlike any other. We first boarded a tour-like wooden boat, which docked by an island so that we could board canoes to maneuver the canal. I was scared Sam might tip us over, watching with wariness as he laughed hysterically every time the boat rocked. Mom said this was like a ride at Disney World.

At Disney, the snakes were fake.

We left the boats and ventured onto an island. It looked deserted, but people were making, packaging, and shipping coconut candy, all from this remote part of the Mekong Delta. We shopped through their embroidered fabric and ate in their restaurant. Just after lunch though, Sam truly lost it—erupting into a fit of screams I could not soothe or calm.

When Uncle saw Sam acting up like this, he threatened to leave him on the island if he didn't stop. Sam became hysterical. Dave told me to do something about it, but I cried and told him that if I knew what to do, I would have.

I felt so helpless in that moment.

On the boat ride back to the van, Sam screamed and thrashed wildly. He was over-tired and no one could calm him. I decided to try the therapeutic holding we had learned from the attachment specialist, the techniques I had found so much success with when it came to helping Brendan. I held him. He kicked, screamed, spat, and wiggled. I held on and spoke calmly as everyone on the boat held their ears and moved as far away as they could. I held him while he screamed and cried and fought for his life.

It felt like hours, but his little body finally gave way to the exhaustion, and he slept on my chest for the remainder of our off-road adventure.

Finally back in the van, we retraced our way over the bridges, and back to Ho Chi Minh City.

From there, we waited out the days until we would finally be able to go home.

Photos

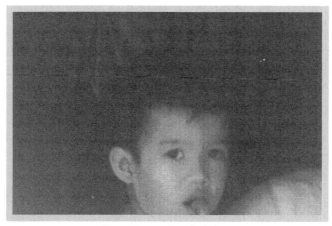

First glimpse of our little boy

First family picture

Boys watching
Beauty and
The Beast

Sam giving water
to his friends

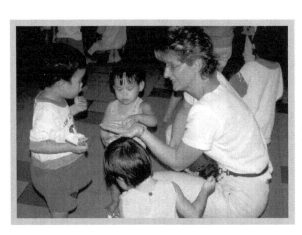

Sharing
crackers

Infant room
at orphanage

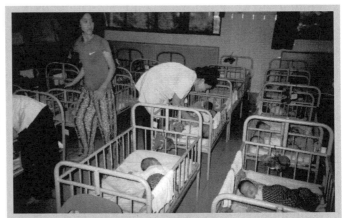

Twin waiting for
adoptive family to
take her home

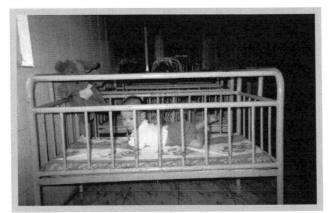

Lunch at
orphanage

Traffic in Ho
Chi Minh City

Canoe in
Mekong Delta

Holding Sam on
long boat ride

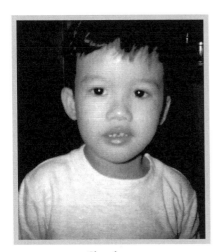

Glazed eyes

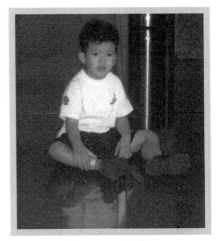

Sam sat on this floor
for long hours

Killing time with another bath

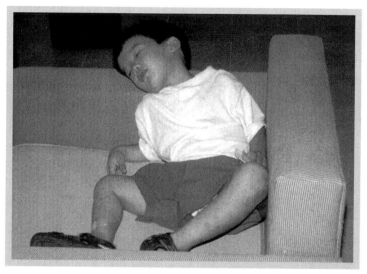

Finally asleep after screaming

Squat pot

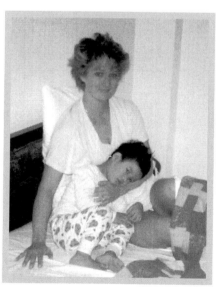

Trying to give comfort in the night

Uncle No
Problem

Flooded
amusement
park on
way back to
orphanage

Soldiers with
kids at zoo

Granny
holding Sam
in van ride
to Soc Trang

Dave holding
Sam outside
orphanage in
Soc Trang

Dave and Sam
eating cereal

Sam waving after we said goodbye at orphanage

First day of school in America

Chapter Nineteen

TWO WEEKS PASSED, but they felt like one year, each day seeming harder and harder to get through. When we finally returned to the airport for our trip home, anxiety surfaced at the recollection of our previous experience and Bob's unintentional separation from our little group. I was dreading anything similar happening again, and simply wanted to get safely on the plane.

The adoption agency had given us many helpful tips for our travel, but had forgotten to inform us about the names on passports. Our new son's passport listed his American name, Samuel Bihn Quang O'Toole, while his visa listed his Vietnamese name. The ticketing agents wanted the visa and passport to match exactly, a huge roadblock in our attempts to leave. Home felt closer than ever, but now we had a huge problem.

Thankfully, a kind worker with a heart for children stepped in and negotiated on our behalf, somehow working out the details so that we were allowed to board our flight.

None of the vehicles we had transported Sam in prior to this flight had been equipped with seat belts. Now that he was on the plane, I knew I needed to make a decision as to whether to fight this battle. My imagination helped me decide, as I pictured Sam running up and down the aisles, pushing all the buttons and screaming for the next 30-some hours.

I buckled him in.

Sam hated being restrained with a passion. I held my hand over his buckle for the duration of that first two-hour flight. He pinched me, hit me, spit at me, and whined the entire time. We flew during naptime, but he did not want to sleep. My hand turned red and hurt immensely, but he stayed in his seat.

In Hong Kong, we walked on the moving sidewalk to get out some energy. Sam enjoyed playing in the drinking fountain. I sat utterly exhausted and overwhelmed as I watched him soak both his sleeves.

It was in this airport where a sickening thought washed over me. The stress and exhaustion and fear all combined, such that for a fleeting moment I thought about what would happen if I just left him there. What if we went to the bathroom, and I just walked out as soon as he entered the stall? Surely a worker would discover him and recognize him as a Vietnamese orphan. They would get him back to Vietnam where he felt safe, and he would resume the life he had always known. He wouldn't scream anymore. He wouldn't cry. He would be happy, and I would be able to breathe.

The thought lasted for only a moment, and I immediately hated myself for having it. I didn't *want* to do this, but the exhaustion had overtaken my thinking.

The trans-Pacific flight came next. After a long layover, we took off on the 11-hour leg of our trip home. We started off pretty well, with my hand over Sam's buckle. I removed it shortly into the flight and Sam didn't try to escape. A few hours later, he fell asleep. Relief washed over me as I realized that we could now all rest. But something must have startled him about five hours into the journey. The flight attendants had turned off the lights, resulting in total silence… maybe.

The screaming started immediately and with a fury. A scream followed each breath, with no rests in between. The volume increased as the sleeping passengers around us all woke and turned to stare. With my upper-middle class, white family upbringing, I had never faced discrimination based on looks. I faced it now. My blonde hair stood out as I surveyed all the dark locks on board, staring back at me as the one who did not belong. Even my mom and brother had black hair. As far as I could tell, I was the only blonde on the entire flight. If the screaming kid sitting next to me didn't make me stand out, my hair certainly did.

Heads turned in disgust and frustration. One flight attendant had the dreaded job of intervening on behalf of all the passengers. She had such a sweet disposition and wanted to help so badly. She gave Sam milk, a stuffed giraffe, food, slippers—the works—yet the screaming continued.

She implored me to do something. I did my best to explain that he didn't know me well and would scream only louder if I tried to hold him or intervene. After the longest hour of my life, he finally quieted down. I think it was only because he wore himself out.

After this, he climbed around between my mom and I, wetting his pants while sitting on my mom's lap. Thankfully, I had channeled my inner Girl Scout in packing with preparation for the flight. He went through all three outfits I had packed for this trip.

During the layover in San Francisco, we bought food from Panda Express. Sam had tried only a limited number of food items during his short life, and we didn't want to introduce new things to his digestive system too soon, particularly not with another flight to go. That turned out not to really matter though. Even though he loved rice and we knew he needed food, he threw everything we gave him on the floor. Later we discovered that the Jasmine rice he knew and loved from the orphanage smelled and tasted different from the long grain rice we ate in America. At the time though, we didn't realize this distinction.

That last flight came as such a relief. He fell asleep as we took off and didn't budge until I carried him off the plane. We arrived just after midnight, greeted by about 20 family members and friends holding up signs and balloons. At that point, it became clear that Sam remembered Bob, Brendan, and Katie. He seemed genuinely glad to see them. Dressed in little red sweat pants that were soggy from his last round of wetting, he ran towards them and his pants dropped around his ankles. Instead of getting upset, he laughed a hearty laugh.

I so enjoyed seeing him happy. I fell into Bob's arms after all the greetings. My exhaustion permeated my body and mind. I had nothing left, not emotionally or physically. I felt like I could have slept for the next week and still might not catch up.

But that wasn't all. Feeling the love and affection from Brendan and

Katie, I realized how much my emotions had been depleted from the last two weeks of being rejected and physically challenged.

I felt totally hollowed out, a deficit in my reserves that I was now desperate to build back up so that I could be the parent all of my children truly needed and deserved.

Chapter Twenty

W E ARRIVED AT our home about 2:00 a.m. and set up a mattress for Sam in our bedroom. We knew he must be terrified and thought it would help if he at least knew where we were when he woke up. His room in the orphanage had contained about 40 children, so we didn't want to leave him alone—certainly not on this first night. He didn't sleep well, and I didn't sleep at all. He woke up throughout the night and screamed, just as he had in Vietnam.

Brendan and Katie played with him during the day, and he appeared more at ease when they were nearby. After one weekend of family time, however, the kids had to return to school and Bob had to return to work the following Monday. It was now up to Sam and me to figure this thing out by ourselves. I didn't know what to do with him. I still felt so tired and we struggled with communication. I was honestly not looking forward to being alone with him at all.

That, of course, made me very sad. This was my son. I didn't want to feel like this.

I cooked rice for him, but he didn't want it. He ate eggs and fruit, if I warmed the fruit to room temperature. I noticed he winced in pain if he ate anything cold. His broken teeth must have exposed the nerves, and it reminded me of all the doctors' appointments I needed to make for him.

After a few nights of lying awake, simply waiting for his screams, I began to panic. I told myself I still had five hours. Four hours. Three. I couldn't breathe. It would just be a few more hours before everyone left, leaving Sam and me alone for another day. Another day of screaming and hitting and crying and feeling like I couldn't connect with my own child.

This child I didn't know at all.

I tried to stifle my tears, but I was just so scared. This wasn't how it was supposed to be.

One night, at Bob's urging, I went to my mother's house in an attempt to rest there. I drank hot tea, took a bath, and tried to sleep in her guest room. We thought that maybe if I didn't have any responsibilities, and didn't have to worry about Sam, I could close my eyes and fall asleep. And maybe after feeling well rested, I could find my bearings once more and remember how to do this whole parenting thing.

Instead, I lay awake all night.

Before our trip home from Vietnam, Bob had moved nearly every valuable item in our home out of Sam's reach. He had boxed it all up and put it in the basement, removing any temptation for our newest family member to seek and destroy. Yet still, I felt anxiety about everything. I was scared to take my eye off him for even a second. I had no trust or faith in him or myself. Everyone thought it was jet lag, and that it would eventually fade.

That was not the case.

I scheduled an appointment with Dr. Fuller. Bringing along our newest son, Dr. Fuller asked how things were going. I talked about Sam not sleeping, but he stopped me and asked about my sleep.

He said, "You are in crisis. You are exhausted and drained and you won't be able to deal with anything until we get you some sleep. Sleep deprivation is far more harmful than you might realize—you need some rest. That's where we need to start."

I explained that I had tried some over-the-counter sleep aids, but they hadn't helped. So he placed a call to my doctor, who called in a prescription for a muscle relaxant. The night I tried this new medication, Bob had to go out of town for a business trip. The thought of him leaving me alone with the kids terrified me, and I asked if he could get someone else to go. I begged, my tears on the brink of erupting as I looked up at my husband with the whimper of a child. "Please. Please don't go." He had no choice. There was no one else. He had to go. So I put on a brave face and tried to pretend that the threat of his absence didn't make me feel as though I was going to fall off a ledge.

I tried the muscle relaxant that night. Not only could I still not sleep, but now I felt paralyzed. All night, I lay awake, unable to move and fully aware that if something happened, I wouldn't be able to respond. This only made the panic worse, particularly when Sam started in on his screams and I couldn't even convince my body to leave the bed. It wasn't as if he would have allowed me to comfort him anyway, but there we were—him screaming and me feeling as though I might as well be.

The next day, the doctor called in a prescription for an anti-depressant. When I picked it up, the pharmacist asked if I knew it might make me sleepy. The corners of my mouth turned upward even though I was too tired to even respond. But that night, I slept.

The shortest verse in The Bible is "Jesus wept." Two words, carrying such meaning for me, because I knew he understood feelings of grief.

I will forever feel as though the most powerful phrase in my life is "I slept."

I still felt overwhelmed, but not so terrified after a few good nights of sleep. The anti-depressants started to take their hold, helping me to feel more capable of taking on these new challenges. I remained on the medication for about six months to help with our transition. We went back to the counselor and talked about Sam's sleep—still better than mine, despite the fitful nature. We discussed that even though we knew we were safe for Sam, he did not feel secure. We might as well have been aliens, for all he knew. We smelled weird, ate funny food, lived in a house he didn't understand, our language sounded like babbling, and most importantly, we weren't "home" to him.

Dr. Fuller asked what his sleeping conditions were like in the orphanage. I described the small beds with the rungs and he said, "Oh, you mean, like a crib?" He told me to set up a crib in a room away from Bob and me, turn on a nightlight and some white noise, shut the door, and leave him alone. He needed time to calm down, away from us. That night, we set him up in his own room just as Dr. Fuller had suggested, and, for the first time, he slept peacefully.

We started to communicate simply with a made up sign language. Sam would put his hand to his mouth when hungry and gesture with a make-believe glass if he needed a drink.

During his first month home, I took him to have a complete physical at the pediatrician's office. They weren't sure if he had ever been immunized, so they gave him all the shots he may have missed. A few days later, I got a call from the Department of Health telling me that his blood had tested positive for Hepatitis B. They thought I would be shocked or saddened, but that had been the one accurate thing in the medical report given to us by the adoption agency. It was the one thing we already knew.

We visited an orthopedist to look at his foot, which had terrible scarring of unknown origin. The doctor told us that Sam's birth mother had probably bound her belly to prevent her family from knowing about her pregnancy. This may have caused Sam to have a clubfoot, which had probably been repaired by a missionary doctor. He said whoever did the surgery had done a great job and we didn't need to do anything else.

The trip to the dentist turned out to be the most difficult for us all. As soon as we walked into the office, Sam started screaming and tried to get away. He screamed in terror. Visits to the other doctors hadn't caused this kind of response, and he didn't yet understand what a dentist did, so where had this reaction come from? The dentist did the best she could to calm him and conduct a very short, non-intrusive exam. She told us that Sam had one missing tooth, and she wondered if maybe someone had pulled it without the use of Novocain.

It certainly explained his aversion to this place.

She thought the smell of her office caused his strong reaction. She could tell he needed surgery for all the repairs that would be necessary, so a few weeks later she did all the work under a general anesthetic. While he was asleep, she did a full exam, cleaned his teeth, deadened eight nerves, filled eight cavities, and capped eight teeth. He was out for three hours. After he recovered, Sam's sensitivity went away and he could finally eat any food he wanted, without concern for temperature.

His little tummy needed time to get used to the variety of foods he experienced in his new culture.

I called Child Find, an agency that deals with kids who had learning delays. At this point, we really didn't know the level of Sam's intelligence, but he seemed to be struggling to pick up English. After he had been with us for a few months, we set him up for a battery of tests. I watched as they performed the tests and found how difficult simple tasks were for him.

They placed two blocks on the table before stacking a third atop them both. Next, they gave him three blocks and showed him they wanted him to do the same. He couldn't figure out how to stack one block on top of two others though. It seemed like an impossible task to him. They explained this had to do with his spatial relations. Because he had spent so much of his life in a crib and wasn't able to crawl and climb at the appropriate time, his development lagged.

Children learned the concepts of "under," "over," "next to," and "on top of" by physically performing those actions. He had never been given the chance to do that, so he hadn't learned these concepts. He walked up stairs with the same foot going first, and the other always following. I had to teach him to alternate his feet, and even that took a long time.

He didn't know how to climb the ladder of a slide, or how to slide down once he reached the top. He hadn't learned how to swing. There were so many things that we just assumed all kids knew how to do, until we realized they were learned behaviors that Sam had missed. When we received the test results after a few weeks, we sat in stunned silence as we reviewed the depressing results.

In all categories, Sam had scored below the 1st percentile in his age group. We had expected him to score low, because of the language barrier, but this news stunned us. We started to wonder if he would ever catch up. Would he be able to learn English? Read? Ride a bicycle?

Would he ever be able to function independently?

It felt like such a low blow. We had been trying so hard to help him fit in, but now we were learning that his problems were far more severe than we thought. I had a difficult time accepting and dealing with this turn of events. We began a grieving process of sorts.

We had to grieve the child we thought we would receive, so that we could love the child we actually had.

Four-year-old Sam started preschool in the spring, alongside other three-year-old children. They assigned him to special education, and we hoped it would help him catch up. I felt such a relief to have him attending school a few hours per week.

I had been working for The Pampered Chef for seven years now, with a home-based business that had expanded rapidly. At the time of Sam's adoption, I held the title of Senior Director. My responsibilities included holding about six shows per month, training new consultants, coaching current consultants, writing a monthly newsletter, and holding two training meetings per month.

One month after returning from Vietnam, I told Bob I could not do my job and raise this child at the same time.

He gave me wise advice: "Cut back on everything you can, and focus on the things only you can do. Delegate as much as possible and spend time on the long-term health of the business."

I did exactly that.

I gave away all the shows I had scheduled, to people I had trained. I did some coaching, but cut back. My weekly activities now included a trip to the attachment counselor an hour away. We hired Dr. Fuller to come to our home and observe Sam in his own environment as well.

I wanted help with how to handle him while I needed to work, even if that only turned out to be a few hours per week. He didn't do any-thing to cause trouble while I talked on the phone, but he just sat on the floor and stared blankly at me. Dr. Fuller made a square on the floor out of masking tape, a bit behind my chair. Then he told me to choose two toys to put in a box that would also reside there. He explained that Sam needed to stay in the square while I made one phone call. He could play with the toys in the square, or just sit, but this way I would at least know that he was safe.

We tried it out. Sam didn't leave the box and I was able to focus because I didn't have to see him staring at me. He could still sit and stare, of course, but it no longer affected me. Sam had the choice to play or to sit, but I could do what needed to get done.

One phone call at a time—that was our solution.

In between phone calls, I played with him. I would get down on the floor and engage him with those toys. I realized I spent a great deal of time playing with Sam, and when I was there, he usually played as well. But if I needed him to play alone for a few minutes while I made those calls, he just sat and stared at me. He didn't cry or fuss, but he also didn't seem to know how to play by himself.

I started to grow anxious about those stares again. It felt as if he needed to look at me for him to be okay. But I couldn't make him okay. It was too much pressure. I felt like he wanted me to fix him, or to make everything better, and I didn't know how.

I learned later that at around two years old, children start to realize they are separate from their mothers. They use her as a "home base." If they are securely attached, they learn to leave her side to explore the world, but they come back to her when they need comfort or support. Sam never had this, so he needed the reassurance of my presence at all times. He didn't feel comfortable in his own skin.

We spent many hours doing attachment exercises. When he became upset, I held him close, stroked him, and told him I loved him and that he was safe. He stopped the behavior, but never seemed to respond to my affection the way Brendan had so many times before. Instead, Sam simply checked out and refused to get angry. Many times, he just fell asleep. I learned that if he didn't express anger in a healthy way, it would come out through controlling behaviors later on. He manipulated, lied, came between people, and struggled for control.

I tried to provide a safe place for him to get that anger out without hurting himself or anyone else. Sam stared without any emotion for as long as I could hold out. I stuck with it for years, trying to break through, but Sam had such a need to be in control that he could outlast me even if I continued forever. There was so much pent up aggression and sadness. His aggression tended to come out in little, manipulative, annoying ways that were hard to catch and explain.

Did he really just run headfirst into the garage door?

Was he trying to annoy us?

He said what to you?

Is he setting us up against each other?

Is he deliberately starting an argument between Brendan and Katie?

This strange behavior caused us to question everything about our parenting and sanity. Were we really seeing what we thought we saw?

Chapter Twenty-One

SEPTEMBER 11, 2001. That date is recognizable to each of us, and like most people, I remember distinctly what we were doing. Katie had a field trip scheduled with her first grade class. Sam had a horrible morning and came to the point where I needed to restrain him physically with a holding time. I held him on my bed and told him he would be alright.

"I am the mom and you are the little boy. I know you used to have to take care of everything, but now you have a mommy. Little boys need mommies to care for them. It's okay to let me be the mommy and for you to be the little boy."

With Sam screaming and raging as I held him, Bob called to tell me a plane had just hit the World Trade Center. I remember picturing a small plane crashing. I didn't have time to think about it. As I held Sam, I needed to also help Katie pack her lunch. She waited patiently in the kitchen while Sam acted totally out of control, screaming, spitting, thrashing, and crying.

I started giving instructions to Katie over Sam's screams, and calmly told her to get out two pieces of bread and the peanut butter and jelly. I talked her through the steps as she assembled her own sandwich. I knew she had helped me make lunches many times before, but something ached inside of me as I had to leave her alone to make her own sandwich now.

I wanted to be the same hands-on mom she had always known.

I wanted to be part of all the little things in each of my children's lives.

But now, Sam took up so much of my time and attention, often making it impossible for me to be the kind of mother I wanted to be to the other two.

I couldn't help her because I had to hold my other child who wanted nothing to do with me. He spit in my face as he tried to get away. I saw the second plane hit the second tower after Katie left for school, while I was still holding my screaming child. The towers fell and I sat totally shocked and horrified. I realized as all of this happened that my own little crisis was preventing me from relating to the outside world.

I hadn't even kissed Katie "goodbye."

As our nation struggled, my strength crumbled. I felt our family falling apart. I didn't believe that anything we were trying was helping Sam, but I knew that Sam was destroying the rest of us.

There were so many days when Bob would be getting home from work just as I was hitting my limit. Sam would rush to the door at his return, acting as if everything had gone as it should. For a long time, Bob didn't understand the relationship between Sam and me. He didn't understand my overwhelming frustration.

Sam acted like a different child with Bob around, and there were times when I was sure he was trying to come between us. He played us against each other. It was so hard to believe that a small child had the power to manipulate adults in this way, but he did.

During this time we continued counseling, and we knew what behavior to look for. Sometimes we caught it, but due to the covert method of delivery, there were times when it slipped by us. At four years old, Sam was incredibly adept at manipulation. One day, at the height of my own personal feelings of defeat, I went to visit Dr. Fuller on my own.

As I sat in his office, trying to explain what was happening without sounding completely paranoid or delusional, he stopped me. "You feel like you are being abused," he said, "because you are."

A strange relief washed over me. Was he telling me I wasn't crazy? That this was real, and I wasn't making it all up in my head? In having my torment at least acknowledged, I suddenly felt as though I could breathe a little more.

Talking to Sam didn't work. I had tried everything I could to show him our relationship as mother and child. He would not give up his control or trust me. So we had to try something else, and that started with learning more about Sam's condition.

It turns out that early trauma can cause Post Traumatic Stress Disorder (PTSD) in some institutionalized children. The safety of his current situation didn't register with the tumultuous emotions. In some ways, he was still back at that orphanage—fighting for survival each and every day. He saw danger around every corner. Just as a war veteran struggled with adjusting to the calm of their life at home, Sam couldn't accept that he no longer needed to be constantly on guard.

For his first three and a half years of life, Sam knew instinctively that he controlled whether he lived or died. He literally felt that everything he did was a matter of survival. We could not help him believe we could protect him, and he wouldn't allow himself to trust us.

Even through many examples of our protection and love for him, he would not relax his survival mode.

One of the first things Dr. Fuller encouraged us to do was take a vacation, just Bob and me. He explained that we needed to reconnect as a couple so that we could take a united front in facing Sam's issues. He also believed I needed to get away for my own health, saying that breaks were necessary when a family was under this much stress. I needed it, he told me, so that I could be the best mom possible.

We wound up booking a trip to Cancun, Mexico, that I had earned through The Pampered Chef. It was an all-inclusive vacation at a luxury resort. One of the things I loved most was to sit on the beach and read or stare at the ocean, and this was going to be the perfect opportunity to receive the rest I was feeling so deprived of.

My mom took the kids and Bob and I had an amazing time parasailing, lying on the beach, and getting the rest we both needed. We reconnected and made our marriage a priority again. It was blissful.

When we returned, however, we discovered that while Sam and Katie had been fine, Brendan had melted down during our absence. He had destroyed his room, dumped his mattress on the floor, overturned his desk, tore apart his modular bookcase, and thrown his books to the ground. Then he had "run away," hiding in the bushes while my mom had searched frantically for him.

He explained that he had suddenly grown afraid that Bob and I were going to die and he would have to live with Granny. He loved his Granny, but the thought of us dying made him want to sabotage his room. In his panicked state, he thought that if he behaved poorly, we wouldn't be able to die because Granny wouldn't be willing to take him. In his then nine-year-old mind, this made perfect sense.

This incident showed a great example of fear, a lack of trust, and how a combination of the two could drive people—especially children—towards self-defeating behavior, or sabotage.

What good did all that destruction do Brendan? *It didn't do him any good.*

Was it logical? *No.*

Why did he do it? *He needed to control something.*

Talking to Brendan in the days that followed revealed to us how much the stress of our changing family dynamics had been weighing on our children.

We had been so focused on fixing Sam, not even realizing that Brendan was feeling more and more scared and disconnected.

Was our family crumbling like the towers in New York?

Chapter Twenty-Two

*A*s TIME MARCHED on, we struggled with every area of life: what clothes to wear, what food to eat, cleaning, behavior, following directions—everything. Sam seemed to be experiencing all kinds of anxiety and constantly plotted to stir up confrontation between different family members. He would even talk incessantly through movies, to the extent that we couldn't ever really relax and enjoy ourselves. He had such difficulty learning new things that directions needed to be repeated literally hundreds of times. He would ask the same questions again and again, sometimes seemingly out of spite.

Sam refused to look me in the eye. When I asked him a question, he looked away. "Sam, look into my eyes," I'd request. He'd turn his head and assume the position of looking in my eyes, but he couldn't actually do it. Children with attachment issues have difficulty with vulnerability, and eye contact felt too powerless. He looked either at my nose or my forehead.

He looked right through me.

Many of these things may sound like normal family occurrences, but it was the intensity and consistency with which they were displayed that was so much higher than with other children. Daily now, I felt like I was losing my family. We had known things would be different with Sam in our home, but we had never thought this little boy would have the power to control so many aspects of our lives.

Brendan's disconnection continued to grow as well. One night when he was misbehaving during dinner, I told him he needed to stop it.

"We don't act like that in this family," I said.

His response startled me: "I'm not part of this family. I wasn't born from your tummy!"

Thankfully, I didn't have to think too long before responding, "Dad and I were married into this family, Katie was born into this family, and you and Sam were adopted into this family. You don't have to have come from my tummy to be my family. And in this family, we don't act like that, so stop it or go to your room."

God must have put those words into my mouth that day, because I don't think I could have come up with a response like that on my own.

School took a lot out of Sam physically, mentally, and emotionally. We came to understand that he never needed help with English as a second language (ESL), because he didn't know language to begin with. Before we ever went to get him, we had found people who spoke Vietnamese who we thought might be able to work with him, but it turned out to be wholly unnecessary.

Once we were at home, I called these friends when Sam said the word "Baqua" several times over the course of a few days. I explained what he said, and what he was doing at the time he spoke it. Usually, it was when he was in the bath and got soap in his eyes. He would pinch his little eyes together and then say it. "Baqua."

None of my Vietnamese-speaking sources knew what the word meant though. I asked if it could mean "Ouch, my eyes hurt," "help me," or "hand me a towel." But no such word existed.

In the kitchen, he would reach toward the cupboards and said, "Munay." My sources said this word didn't exist either, but cutely conjectured that perhaps he was looking for "money." It remained a mystery.

He knew how to count to 10, and understood enough to follow a few commands, but didn't seem to have any conversational language. We learned that in institutions children sometimes made up language with each other that the adults around them didn't understand. I don't think the adults took the time to teach conversational language, so whatever the children picked up, they learned from each other.

Before Sam joined our family, we purchased a pop-up tent trailer to go camping. Bob and I loved to tent camp before we had children. The mountains were so calming and we both felt closer to God out in nature. We tried to tent camp with Brendan and Katie, but the dirt got everywhere and it made my job so much harder that it was difficult to have much fun. Thus, the pop-up trailer joined our family.

After that, we enjoyed camping again. We had running water, beds off the ground, and heat—what's not to love? We upgraded to a larger pop-up when Sam came into our lives.

For years, we had spent Memorial Day weekend camping in Rocky Mountain National Park. This year we decided to continue the tradition, bringing Sam along with us for the first time. We thought he would enjoy the outdoors, and Estes Park was close by, a tiny town with a fun little adventure park that consisted of bumper cars, a huge racing slide, and go karts. It had always been a favorite place for the kids, and we hoped to create some new and lasting family memories.

Sam's birthday fell over the holiday weekend, so he enjoyed opening presents in the camper and getting to ride the go-karts. Everything seemed to be going well, all the kids laughing and smiling with excitement at everything we did.

One night we sat in the camper talking, asking the kids what they each wanted to do when they grew up. Brendan said he wanted to do something creative, like writing, filming, or building things. Katie wanted to sing, dance, and perform. Sam said he wanted to help hungry kids get enough to eat, and help children who had problems falling asleep. It was a glimpse at the thoughtful boy we knew resided within him, and I felt my heart melting towards my youngest son on that trip.

Life for Sam had been difficult. Things most people took for granted did not come easily for him. He somehow already seemed to know that secondary schooling would not likely be in his future. But this did not mean he didn't have a future, or that God did not have a plan for his life.

Most days, Bob and Sam got up at dawn together. Bob had an early work schedule and his body didn't adjust on the weekends. Sam had simply been an early riser since we met. When he first learned my name, he would lay in his room at 4:30 in the morning yelling "Ma!" "Ma!"

For a few weeks in the beginning, I went every time he called and got him up. As my lack of sleep caught up with me, I told him he needed to stay in his bed until wake up time. He still called for me, but now I would tell him to go back to sleep. I couldn't start the day that early. Not anymore.

On Saturdays, Bob and Sam ran errands together. This became their father/son time. They went to Wal-Mart, McDonald's, and Starbucks. The manager knew them so well that when Bob went alone, he asked about Sam. This time gave the rest of us a chance to sleep a little later and wake up in peace without Sam screaming or crying. I truly appreciated this gift of sleep my husband gave us, and the special quality time he was granting to our youngest boy.

With time, we all began falling into a routine.

Sam slowly started picking up English. It was as if a light bulb went on. He suddenly seemed to grasp that we were actually saying something that made sense, not just speaking gibberish. After that, he picked up a few words and short phrases. Every day he asked, "What time…Da…home…work?" *What time will Dad be home from work?*

He always wanted to know where everyone was, what time they would be home, and especially what would be served for the next meal.

As the years passed by, we encouraged Sam's love of sports. He played on a recreational basketball league several years in a row. He amazed us with his basketball skills. He had come to us with physical deficiencies, but when he played competitive ball, his body seemed to know just what to do. It was some of the most natural talent we had ever seen. Bob and I both loved watching him from the stands. His teammates all liked him. He showed compassion if someone got injured, and gave support whether his friends played well or poorly. His coaches commented on his sense of team spirit and ability to encourage all the players.

We enjoyed taking him to Denver Nuggets and Colorado Rockies games when Bob's company gave him extra tickets. He usually fell asleep about halfway through the games, but they were fun times where he always seemed excited and involved.

We taught Sam to ski one winter by using a harness around his body. A

10-foot rope led from Sam to Bob, and Bob could control Sam's speed from behind. Sam was able to ski on his own, but Bob made sure he didn't get out of control or too close to other people or obstacles. Sam did well, and loved the challenge.

Since one foot and lower leg didn't have as much strength or control as the other, he struggled from time to time with his clubfoot. But he learned to adjust for this, and embraced any opportunity to be physical.

As those first few years went by, we were able to identify most of his issues. It took time, as there weren't even true assessments that accounted for his change of culture, language deficits, and becoming part of a family, but certain things started to become clear. He definitely had trouble with auditory processing skills, which showed up in the way that he understood what people said to him, but he could not formulate a response. He had a clear delay in his expressive speech as well. It frustrated all of us, because we knew he understood what we said, but he couldn't think of the words to answer simple questions.

In school, teachers asked him questions that we all knew he understood, but he couldn't verbalize a response. School staff had to come up with different ways to test him, and it was a constant struggle to evaluate his true learning level.

The eye doctor couldn't use the normal test for preschoolers when he first came to us, either. He showed Sam pictures of planes and houses, but Sam couldn't identify them or answer the questions accurately. He wore glasses from around the age of five on, but his prescription changed many times as his language and ability to express himself improved. The eye doctor was finally able to give a correct assessment when Sam could tell him which picture was the "plane" or the "house."

We took Sam to a great chiropractor for about six years. Dr. Boykin kept his hips aligned, which was necessary due to the clubfoot. He adjusted his spine each week, and assured us that this care would help him as he grew and his bones changed. Sam loved him, but didn't like the adjustments. He couldn't say chiropractor, so Dr. Boykin became the "cracker-backer." I thought the name was cute, and it seemed to fit in a way that made these visits less anxiety-inducing for Sam.

As he settled into life with us, we started to realize he was lying about really mundane things. Dr. Fuller called this "crazy lying." As an example, he might come out of the kitchen with cookie crumbs on his face and the lid off the cookie jar. Sam knew he could eat cookies, so he didn't have to worry about getting into trouble. But if I asked him if he ate a cookie, he lied about it and got upset if I questioned him any further. He protested, "Why don't you believe me?" He lied about little things, like cookies, and big things, like whether he took a knife from the kitchen, or whether he stole money out of my purse.

Many times I questioned myself, my memory, and the harshness of my response. I wondered if he had actually done what I had just observed him doing. He lied so well, and was a master at the art of manipulation. It was only with time that I started to learn to trust my discernment, and realized that if I thought he had lied, he had probably lied.

Dr. Fuller helped us understand the severity of his problematic behavior, explaining that it would only get worse if we didn't do something drastic to stop it.

From that point on, if Sam lied, he had to go to bed at 6:00 p.m. for three days in a row. We observed that the first night he displayed his anger at us by crying and carrying on for a long time. The second night he remained mad, but settled down more quickly. The third night, he realized his fault in the matter and concluded that lying wasn't worth all of this. After several rounds of bedtime at 6:00, his lying was reduced considerably.

Sam liked to talk, a lot. He talked when people were listening, and when they weren't. He talked non-stop in the car, pointing out everything he saw and asking rapid-fire questions. It was a relief to see his language skills growing, and his special education teachers thought he did this because he had learned language so late.

Even at six, seven, and eight years old, he still exhibited the frequent question-asking trademarks of a preschooler. What the teachers didn't understand was that this was a common controlling symptom of RAD—incessant talking and nonsense questioning. Trying to describe this behavior to people who hadn't observed it was always a struggle. How do you explain what you couldn't truly understand yourself?

One such conversation involved several friends, and concerned Jay Cutler, the new Denver Broncos quarterback at the time. Sam gave descriptions of Jay—where he grew up, statistics, how great the Broncos would be with Jay as quarterback. We listened and engaged for several minutes, until the conversation changed. Sam tried to stop the change by going back to Jay Cutler. This happened several times. Our friends listened to Sam, asked a few questions, and showed true interest for several minutes. Sometimes they'd debate about whether Sam thought Jay Cutler could take the Broncos to the Super Bowl, or not. But when they told him they wanted to talk about something else, Sam refused to switch to any other topic.

He wouldn't let anyone else speak.

His Jay Cutler talk kept on going and going until someone got frustrated enough to tell him to be quiet. He started to cry as if no one cared about him or what he wanted to talk about. He didn't understand that not everyone wanted to listen to him talk about Jay Cutler for an hour. Actually, I think he *did* understand, but he wanted to control the situation, even if it meant alienating everyone else.

Sam was so frequently like this. He talked during my phone conversations, he interrupted others while they spoke, he talked during movies, at church, and pretty much during any awake time.

To prevent this from happening in the future, Dr. Fuller suggested that when we watched movies, Sam could either sit with us and watch quietly or he would have to sit on the stairs by himself. He couldn't go to his room to play. He had to sit near us, but out of our hearing. In this way, we could watch and enjoy the movie, but he couldn't do what he wanted.

When kids struggle with RAD, they want to be left alone. They don't believe they need anyone. They want to get sent to their rooms. Dr. Fuller explained that instead of "time-outs," Sam needed "time-in." We didn't want to send him to his room to isolate him further, but we needed him to stop the annoying behavior. This method did help us to start watching movies again, but the truth is, it never did a thing to stop his incessant talking.

We spent thousands of dollars for two separate 24-week sessions of vision therapy prescribed by our eye doctor. He studied extensively on brain function, processing, and eye development. Being raised the way he had been, with limited contact or movement during his early months, Sam's eyesight simply hadn't developed the way it should have. This impacted his processing ability.

I spent an hour each day working specifically on his vision therapy homework with him. This needed to be done on top of his regular homework and life skills training. Adding this into our daily schedules was extremely difficult for the both of us, not just because of the added hour per day, but also because of the energy required to get Sam to do the exercises and remain on task.

I did my best, but life challenged both of us. He didn't want to do the exercises, which required hard concentration. He especially didn't like working hard for me.

The school referred us to an audiologist, and, as I had suspected in Vietnam, Sam had hearing loss in one ear. For several years, it wasn't severe enough to treat. His teacher let him sit in the front row and made sure he looked at her when she spoke. In time, his need for hearing aids grew. He hated wearing them and didn't like for me to put them in. They had to sit exactly in the right spot in his ears or they didn't work. Many times it took me several tries to place them correctly, through his squirming body and escape attempts.

However, he did enjoy personalizing his new hearing aids to show his team spirit: blue for one ear and orange for the other—**Go Broncos!**

We became fast friends with the orthodontist. He had already treated Brendan and Katie, and I'm sure he enjoyed seeing Sam as well. His mortgage payment would be secure for many years to come with this new patient.

The orthodontist quickly discovered that Sam's mouth contained an anomaly. When he looked at the X-rays, he found something totally unique. Sam's adult front tooth consisted of a conglomeration of four teeth fused together. He pulled it, because nothing else would move with that tooth in the way. The doctor seemed like a school kid getting to do the greatest experiment of his life—it was clear he had never seen anything like this before. We were amused that the orthodontist found our son's teeth to be so entertaining and challenging. The X-rays looked like something from a horror movie to me.

During Sam's first dental surgery after we arrived from Vietnam, the dentist had capped eight teeth, including his two front teeth. One of them formed an abscess, and needed to be pulled. The other fell out, so he had no front teeth for two years.

The orthodontist chose to treat Sam using two rounds of braces so he could adjust some of the teeth and prepare others for new arrivals. He hoped this would save time and discomfort with the second round.

He also discovered that Sam's canine and incisor teeth were growing in reverse. During his development, they had somehow switched places. Orthodontists can straighten crooked teeth, but they cannot change the position of teeth once they are set. This caused problems. Canines set the jaw, and we couldn't get the canines to the right place. The orthodontist pulled several more teeth throughout Sam's treatment. At some point, we realized Sam would need to have dental implants to replace the missing teeth.

So many parts of this little boy's body simply did not function the way they should.

Plus, Sam seemed to be a magnet for physical injury...

Chapter Twenty-Three

ONE DAY, I returned from a Pampered Chef show to find Sam cradling his arm at bedtime. He didn't say it hurt, but we knew he had a high tolerance for pain. He and Katie had been playing in the basement when Sam rolled off a beanbag chair onto the floor. He hadn't fallen far or landed hard, but he held his arm as if it really hurt. I asked if he wanted me to take him to the doctor, but he said he was fine. I took him to the doctor in the morning, and they assured me it was not broken, since he could move it without screaming. They didn't even feel the need to give him an X-ray.

It was odd for him to be complaining like this, but I believed them because they were the doctors. The accident happened on a Thursday and I took him to be seen on Friday. By dinner Friday evening, Sam couldn't lift his fork to his mouth. He could not longer move without screaming.

I took Sam to the emergency room at the hospital Saturday morning, and after waiting four hours to be seen, they X-rayed his arm—now obviously broken. By this point, his arm had swollen so much that they could not even cast it. They put him in a sling and told us to have it casted at the doctor's office on Tuesday.

We went camping at a local campground that weekend. The trip had been planned, and the kids all begged us not to cancel it. Sam truly wanted to go. We changed locations to be closer to home, in case Sam's pain worsened. Sunday afternoon he asked if we'd let him play on the playground. We relented and told him to stay on the slide and swings, as Bob and I stood guard. Sure enough, we stood right next to him as he slid off the playground equipment directly onto his arm.

We returned for the "Bronco Blue" cast on Tuesday. It helped ease the pain, and Sam loved having his classmates sign his arm.

And the medical problems continued...

At age seven, the doctor discovered that one of Sam's testicles had not descended. This apparently occurred frequently with boys, but he needed surgery to repair it. The office staff tried to tell us how lucky we were that they found this problem when they did, because after age 10, it could cause infertility problems.

I was frustrated and scared for my little boy. He went through another surgery and healed quickly.

Unfortunately, that was not the end of our medical issues.

In 2004, our country experienced a shortage of flu vaccine doses. Because of Sam's weak immune system and his Hepatitis B, he needed to have a yearly flu shot. I called our pediatrician and asked them to hold a dose for Sam. The receptionist documented my request and said I could bring him in for his vaccine any time.

My son had been through the medical ringer, and I tried my best to spare him from extra suffering. He hated shots, and when we entered the office, he started to cry immediately. We had to wait several minutes before going to the exam room. The nurse came in and started going over the same paperwork we signed with every shot. And at every visit, I saw the "Hepatitis B Positive" warning sticker on the front cover of Sam's medical chart. She said, "Hep B, right."

I nodded, affirming his positive status, and that we were there for a flu shot. I asked her to please give it quickly. The wait caused more panic than the shot, and I wanted it to be over for Sam.

She gave him the injection. "You need to bring him back in two weeks for his second dose."

I was immediately confused. The flu shot only had one dose.

I asked what she was talking about, and she left the room in a panic. I sat alone with Sam crying from the shot, fearfully wondering what was going on. The doctor came into our room soon after and immediately put his arm around me. He told me everything would be okay.

I asked what had happened.

The nurse had given Sam a Hepatitis B immunization. His chart showed him clearly as a carrier of the Hepatitis B virus. The nurse apologized profusely, and the doctor told me it would not harm Sam in any way. Since he already had the disease, the small dose in the vaccine would not impact him. They had basically just given him an unnecessary shot and we would need to come back later for the flu shot.

Sam needed comfort, and I grabbed my belongings and left as fast as I could. I held my tears until Sam went down for a nap. *Why couldn't he get a break? Why was everything so difficult for this child? Why did those to whom I entrusted Sam so often harm him instead of help him?*

The office manager called that afternoon, begging me not to sue them. I had no intention of suing, but I also needed to find a new pediatrician.

Immediately. For Sam's sake.

Chapter Twenty-Four

S O MANY OF the stressors we were facing at home found me turning to Jesus and growing in my relationship with Him. I began to see a common theme between my relationship with Him and my relationship with my kids. God held me close. Sometimes I kicked and screamed, trying to do things my own way. I yelled at Him, blamed Him, and said horrible things to try and hurt Him. He continued to hold me through it all.

Sometimes I struggled so hard to get away that I hurt myself in the process. He often increased His firm grip to remind me that I'm safest in His arms.

All the while, He whispered that He loved me and wanted me to accept His love. He told me He was the Father, I was the child, and He knew what was best for me.

I believe we all have Reactive Attachment Disorder to some degree. I go through phases where I'm stoic and just stare straight ahead and act like God isn't there. I ignore Him, and just live my life as if He didn't exist. When I get my energy back, I fight to have my own way again. I get angry at God and yell at Him. "Why did you take my dad when he lived his life for you? Now my kids won't have a grandpa their whole lives." Sometimes I just want Him to leave me alone. "What good are you if you don't fix the things that are wrong in this world? Why didn't you protect Sam? Why won't you lead us to someone who can help us?"

If life gets too hard, I scream, "Stop it, you're hurting me!"

He continues to love me and hold me close. Finally, I break. I cuddle in close and start to talk to Him, hearing what He wants to say to me. He continues to love me, and finally I say, "I love you, Daddy." Then I *want* to stay close to Him.

As I trust Him more and more, I am able to take in the love He has offered me all along.

I could see it in my own relationship with Jesus, and I tried to remind myself of that every time my boys were fighting my love.

As we all grew in our faith, Bob, Brendan, Katie, and I decided we wanted to be baptized. Sam didn't quite understand, so we held off until he could comprehend what was happening. The next summer as we drove in the car, Sam said, "I wan be baptized." I knew what he meant, but I didn't know if he understood the meaning.

We read in scripture that night how baptism is a sign of the life change that happens when someone chooses to surrender their heart, will, and life to Jesus. We told Sam he would get in a big tub of water in his swimsuit. The pastor would ask him if he wanted to live his life with Jesus in charge instead of doing things his own way. Then he would dunk Sam under the water to show that Sam's way of doing things was over. When he came up out of the water, it meant he wanted to live the way God wanted him to live. I asked Sam if he understood. He told me Jesus lived in his heart and he wanted to live the way Jesus wanted him to live.

Good enough!

We took him to the elders of our church and they interviewed Sam to make sure he understood to their satisfaction. Something amazing happened there: When Sam spoke to the elders, he spoke in perfect English. I was stunned. The broken English and sentence fragments were replaced by strong, cohesive sentences. It was truly amazing.

The same thing happened when our church members gathered to pray in different areas of the building. Our family went into the church office where the pastors studied and prepared sermons. Sam never shied away from speaking, and had no fear of praying. In front of the whole congregation, he prayed something like, "God, please bless the men who lead us through your Word. Give them wisdom as they prepare their message for us." Most adults would have struggled to pray as eloquently as he did. He prayed in perfect English, words that must have been God inspired because when he finished we all stood in awe.

Bob baptized Sam in August 2003.

Chapter Twenty-Five

A COMMON ATTACHMENT ISSUE surfaced each time we went camping. Sam would talk about it the whole week leading up to our trip. "When camping?" "How many day?" But the minute we got to our camping site, he would act bored and tell us he wanted to do something else. He anticipated each moment, but when the time came to do the activity, he wouldn't participate and wanted to do something else.

Our pop-up trailer felt large compared to a tent. But with all five of us sleeping in such close quarters, and Sam snoring fiercely, it made sleep difficult for everyone. With every inhaled breath, he sounded like he might not survive, gasping for air. The exhalation competed in volume. Patience was fleeting when we all felt exhausted from listening to the snoring hour after hour.

In the mornings, Sam woke before the rest of us and could not find anything quiet to do, so he woke up the whole family. We gave him books and toys to play with quietly, we even talked to him about how his lack of respect for our sleep made it difficult to be happy and have fun, but nothing seemed to convince him to play quietly until normal waking hours.

Once we all woke up, someone would inevitably get mad, and then Sam wanted to sleep because he had been up for so long already. It frustrated everyone, and we started to dislike the family activity we had loved for years.

This happened in more areas of our lives than just camping.

When it was just Sam and me in the car during the week, a strange thing started to happen repeatedly. I would open the garage door and drive in, but if I reached the door to the house before Sam did once we were out of the car, he would yell, "Wait, wait!" before I went into the house.

It was as if he was afraid I was going to leave him.

I always tried to make him feel safe, and worked hard to stay with him when we went places. I constantly battled with my own frustration, working hard to ensure he didn't see it. I knew he was afraid, and didn't want him to feel ridiculed. He panicked as if I would abandon him each time we arrived home. I would have understood it more if we were on the way out, and he feared I would leave him behind. But it didn't make sense for this intense reaction to occur in going from the garage to the house.

Once again, I didn't truly understand how he could feel unsafe even though I was doing everything in my power to make him feel safe. I never left without him, but his fear remained. In my continued study, I discovered that kids with RAD need to experience what experts call "felt safety." This means that even though the parents understand the child is safe, until the child actually *feels* safe, they won't trust. It isn't logical, and parents can't talk their children into feeling safe.

I continued to seek out help, going to seminars and consulting with specialists. I also continued therapy with Dr. Fuller for four years. But sometimes, I wanted to get another perspective.

On more than one occasion, I found myself paying a counselor and then spending most of the session explaining RAD to that counselor. It seemed I often knew more than the counselors. After talking, I found I already knew what to do. I just needed support and reminders to do what I already knew. A counselor I saw for my own issues invited me to attend a conference on RAD with her. The only non-counselor in attendance, they questioned me thoroughly during the sessions. I was the only one who had parented a child with RAD, and they wanted to hear of my experiences firsthand.

None of the counselors understood how a child with RAD affected a family, so as the facilitator presented the material, the counselors would ask me to give examples. They asked, "Does it really look like this?" "Do the kids really do that?" "Can you give us an example of this?"

It felt strange to be used as the authority for the people I had hoped to go to for help.

What do you do when you have more training and education than the specialists, and you still can't fix the problem?

What do you do when you find your life slowly slipping away because a little, scared boy does everything in his power to control you, and won't accept your love?

How do you handle his manipulations, button-pushing, and constant stares?

He stared at me as we watched TV or movies, at church, when I talked on the phone, and when I visited with friends. Sometimes when other kids came over to play, Sam remained by my side, his eyes ever focused on me.

I feared I might start going crazy. Maybe I already was.

I couldn't sleep and depression and anxiety overcame me. Katie and Brendan didn't like their friends to come to our house anymore because Sam embarrassed them. He would then leave my side to follow them around and talk incessantly to their friends as he did his brother and sister. At first, their friends allowed him to join in, but they got annoyed with this cute little boy who completely lacked social skills.

Bob and I spent hours trying to teach him how to give and take in a conversation, how to let others talk, how to speak for a few minutes, and then how to be quiet and listen to the other person. None of this information ever transferred to his behavior.

He cried over being left out, so we talked about what it meant to be a friend. We put pictures of people with faces showing different emotions in his room. The special education teacher thought maybe this would help him to read people's expressions so he would know when someone grew tired of his talking. He couldn't read a person's facial expressions or body language accurately.

If someone grew bored, he kept on talking. If they wanted to be alone, he followed them. If they asked him to go away nicely, he refused.

We tried to teach him social etiquette, how to make friends, and how to be respectful. I continuously struggled to balance whether Sam could do what we asked of him, or if he truly couldn't. Was he defiant, or unable?

Brendan seemed to learn how to deal with this sooner than the rest of us. If Sam bothered him, he didn't ask him to leave politely; he screamed, "Go away, Sam!" And Sam went away. He understood direct language much better than polite language.

I tried so hard to help him feel the love we had for him. I scolded Brendan for being rude and I begged the children to include their brother. As I look back though, Brendan wasn't intentionally being rude; he had simply learned to talk to Sam in a way he understood—bluntly, and with no room for confusion.

One particularly grumpy day, Brendan sat on the couch and stared straight ahead. I could tell something was bothering him, so I began to ask a few questions. I wasn't even sure what prompted them myself, but they seemed to flow naturally, fueled by his current attitude.

"Do you ever wonder what it would be like if you were not in our family?" I asked. A tear slid down his cheek. He didn't look at me, but nodded his head. "Do you ever wonder if your birth mom would understand you better than I do?" Another nod. "Maybe she would have loved the same things as you?" Again, a nod. "Do you ever think you would have fit in better there?"

He didn't ever look at me, or bother nodding this time, but I sat on the edge of the couch and rubbed his back. We remained together for some time and seemed to understand each other.

There was so much love there between us. But that didn't mean there wasn't also a huge sense of loss.

Chapter Twenty-Six

*W*HEN THE KIDS were 12, 11, and 8, I earned an Alaskan cruise for our family through The Pampered Chef. This was going to be the trip of a lifetime, for both our kids and us. We were sure of it.

We decided to take our pop-up trailer and camp all the way to Vancouver and back before and after the cruise. We arrived in Missoula, Montana, at 10:00 p.m., the sun still shining bright. That messed with our internal schedules, but we found it humorous nonetheless. Stranger than that, we returned to our room at 2:00 a.m. in Alaska to find the sun still up. The kids thought this was hilarious.

Saying that the two older kids loved the ship is a gross understatement. The cruise line had a great, fully staffed place for kids under 12. They enjoyed continuous activities, snacks, movies, video games, theme nights, and fun staff members. We had a great week, and all the kids loved it. They spent most of their time in the kids' club, but did things separately.

We knew what kind of clothes to pack from the itinerary. I don't know how we did it, but we managed to pack camping clothes, swimsuits, formal wear, winter coats, and everything in between.

We all stayed in one very small room (although we'd been upgraded to a room with a balcony, compliments of Pampered Chef). We found it difficult to store the suitcases due to the small closet. Bob and I shared the main bed, while Katie slept on the fold-out chair, Brendan slept in a bunk that lowered from the ceiling, and Sam slept on the floor on the cushions from Katie's chair. We were very cozy, but because of the level of activities and choices, we could all do our own thing during the day. It was the perfect vacation.

We took a whale-watching excursion that turned out to be the highlight of our trip. The guides had warned us that sometimes they saw whales and sometimes they didn't, so not to get our hopes up too high.

I had just finished reading a book by John Eldredge. He wrote about God loving each one of us, and wanting us to experience His love frequently. John had walked along a coastline after whale season, and a whale had surfaced right in front of him. He felt God sent this gift to remind him of the lengths He would go to show His love for us.

I gathered our family together on the whale-watching boat and we all prayed that God would bring the whales up so we could see them. We told Him we would be appreciative and wanted Him to show off His creation to us.

Not long after, the orcas started surfacing. Several pods surfaced close to our boat, and we loved every moment of it. Our hearts were filled with thanks to God for this little reprieve from our crazy lives. It felt like He knew we needed a break, and the whales were just the things to lift our spirits.

The guides told us they didn't know why this happened, because they hadn't seen many whales all summer. We knew why.

The kids enjoyed the formal dinners on the ship as well. Katie and I went dress shopping before the trip, and she had a beautiful new pink dress to wear—just as she was entering that stage when dressing up and looking nice had started to seem so important. Brendan, Sam, and Bob had matching black tuxes. Bob and Brendan wore black bow ties, and Sam chose a bright red one. They all looked so cute and loved eating the lobster.

Every one of us looks back with fondness on that trip. In fact, our family has enjoyed several cruises together since our inaugural sailing to Alaska.

The ship really did become "our" place, and was one of those rare moments where we felt united and content as a family. All of the kids loved hanging out in the Kid Zone—they didn't stay together, but each found something they enjoyed. Bob and I were able to spend some uninterrupted time as a couple too. A few nights the kids begged to stay in the Kid Zone late, and we enjoyed a romantic dinner for two.

Soon after our Alaskan cruise, however, I sensed God urging me to quit my job. I really enjoyed everything about it, and it gave me a much-needed break from the tension at home, so I didn't want to quit. I felt successful with Pampered Chef. But that nagging voice in my mind wouldn't let up—I was meant to walk away. At home, I felt like a failure as a wife and mother most of the time. I earned great incentives and great pay, and received the accolades my heart yearned for, but only at work. As a mother, no one got too excited when their laundry appeared in their rooms or dinner placed itself on the table. The feeling persisted, despite my protests to God. I prayed that if He wanted me to quit my job, He would take away my passion for it. I truly enjoyed what I did, and I didn't want to feel resentful.

Within a few weeks, I started experiencing problems I had not encountered in my 10 years of business management. My shows started conflicting with family events. Bob scheduled last-minute travel for business when I had a meeting planned. Leads that I had become a pro at signing up for their own businesses didn't pan out. Hosts canceled their shows, or worse, hosted shows with only three or four people in attendance, after I drove an hour to get there.

At this point in my business, my time was valuable, so all of these setbacks frustrated me greatly. My heart didn't love this anymore. I believed that God had answered my prayer, and suddenly I wanted out. Bob and I discussed what to do about this quandary. My escape was disappearing.

I felt I needed to quit. Bob worried about the practical things, like the mortgage. We had moved to a large house on 10 acres. He made good money, but we would need to move again without my income. It took time for us to come to agreement on this issue, and it was difficult. He trusted in me though, and my relationship with God, so we put our house on the market.

For about a month, we had almost no movement on our listing. Bob didn't want me to quit until we sold the house. I felt God wanted me to resign first, and then He would sell the house. As I look back, we needed some lessons in trusting God, but this really stretched our faith.

We finally came to an agreement. In December, I announced that I would be resigning as of January 1, 2005. I shocked the entire team.

No one understood why I wanted to leave such a great, successful business. I didn't quite know how to tell them, "God told me to quit." It felt so awkward. The day after I announced my resignation, we had two competing offers on our house.

When asked, the kids told me they feared losing their allowance and the trips I earned. Brendan said he was afraid we'd end up homeless. One year later, Bob received a huge salary increase and we asked the kids what differences they had noticed since I'd quit. They told us they still got an allowance, and we had been to Guatemala on a mission trip and Hawaii for fun. The only difference: mom stayed home all the time now and they liked having me there.

God had provided, and all we had needed to do was listen and follow His lead.

Chapter Twenty-Seven

ON THE WAY to the dentist one day, Brendan complained about school, as usual. From first grade on, he had started to protest regularly. After school in Brendan's fifth grade year, homework became a focal point of our arguments with him. Many days the homework left with Brendan in his backpack, but never made it to the teacher. It did not come home with him, and we never found out where it ended up.

I spoke with his teachers weekly, and kept him home more and more often, for what we lovingly called "O'Toole School." On days Brendan woke up irritable, argumentative, combative, and flat-out refusing to do what he needed to do to prepare for school, I kept him home. I found that if I held him, had him sit next to me as I worked, or required him to help me clean the kitchen, soon his gentle heart and pleasant attitude would re-emerge.

As the day went on, he had plenty of time to get his schoolwork done. He did it well, and with enthusiasm. It was much more pleasant for all of us (teachers, other students, Brendan, and me) if I kept him home on these days. He felt detached, and needed time with me that he couldn't get at school.

I had just quit my job, and we were preparing for our move to Parker, Colorado. I asked Brendan what ideas he had that would help him enjoy school more. He could switch to a different public school, or try another charter school. I had no income, but I told him we could look into a private school as well. He blurted out, "I want to be home schooled," and Katie followed enthusiastically with, "Me too!"

This thought terrified me. I knew how to teach music, but didn't know what would be required of me to teach every subject.

We had adopted Sam as Katie entered first grade. I stayed home with Sam through two years of preschool and two years of kindergarten. Now, as Sam was preparing to go to school all day, the other kids wanted me to stay home with them as their teacher? I had been home with at least one child for 10 years, and I looked forward to having some time for myself. I told them I would pray about it. And once again, I felt God's words telling me this was why He had wanted me to quit The Pampered Chef.

It looked like Brendan and Katie's wishes were going to be answered.

It seemed like everywhere I went, the conversation turned to home schooling. I went to a party and struck up a conversation with a woman in line for food. Did we know each other? She asked if I belonged to her home school group. Other friends talked about home schooling every time we got together.

My plan had never included home schooling, but as I started to look into it, I found a curriculum that excited me. Maybe this would be productive and fun after all!

I told Brendan and Katie I would home school them for one year, and we would evaluate how it went. After that time we would make decisions on a year-by-year basis. They agreed, and I started home schooling my two older children that fall. We all loved it!

There were days we read a great book, and at stopping time the kids would beg me to continue. Sometimes we read the entire book in one day, Brendan and Katie dressed in jammies, petting their cats, and snuggling close to me. It was a freedom that allowed us to follow passions from day to day, making learning exciting for them once more. It also gave us much needed time alone, without Sam.

I knew Sam needed the special help he got through public school, so I felt good keeping him there. He desperately needed the social interaction. But he frequently questioned why Katie and Brendan got to stay home for school and he didn't, so after two years of schooling them, I checked into resources for schooling a special needs child at home.

Looking back, I recognize that I pressured myself into this decision out of guilt. At the time, I reasoned that I didn't want Sam to feel different from Brendan and Katie. Other families home schooled special needs children successfully, so surely I could too. But in retrospect, I should have listened to my gut. He needed more help than I was prepared to give.

That fall turned into the worst schooling experience for all of us. Brendan started attending a home school high school two days a week, but Katie and Sam stayed home full time with me.

As Katie remembers it, I left every chance I got and made her watch Sam. I remember making sure I took time each week for bible study and lunch with a friend, but she felt as though I had dumped all of my responsibilities on her. Maybe I did. I know it had never been my intention to make her feel that way, and I don't remember it that way myself, but perception is reality, and her perception is that things changed that year. Drastically. I can look back now and understand that if Sam was too much for me to handle, I certainly shouldn't have put Katie in the position to watch him regularly.

She saw my exhaustion. Sam's consistent need for attention wore on everyone. In eighth grade, the burden of Katie's own schoolwork and her perceived duty to help Sam with his schooling overwhelmed her. Katie started to resent me, and her problems with Sam intensified.

I struggled enough to parent Sam, without the added burden of teaching him. He did not want me to parent him, and he definitely did not want me to teach him. He said he did, but when it came time for school, he fought with everything in him to do the work slowly, poorly, or not at all.

Every day challenged our family more and more.

Once a month, our home school group had a "Presentation Day." This gave the kids a chance to give a speech, perform a dance, sing, play an instrument, act, or share something they had learned, in a public forum.

Sam watched the first few months, and then wanted to participate. He signed up to read a Psalm from The Bible. At this point, Sam spoke with broken English and read very slowly. He needed courage to stand up in front of about one hundred people to read an entire Psalm.

He dressed up for the occasion and combed his hair. He stood in front of the crowd and read almost perfectly from his children's Bible. He did so well, tears ran down my cheeks. My pride swelled, as if he had just sung the national anthem before the Super Bowl.

When he finished, parents gave "constructive criticism." I read the few complimentary comments to Sam and threw the rest away. One mom said he should have memorized the text.

Are you kidding me?

Obviously, she had no idea it had taken him an entire month to be able to read through the whole Psalm as it was.

Another said he should have tucked in his shirt. Sam had worn khaki pants with a collared shirt that he left un-tucked, just like the pastor at church. He had laboriously selected his outfit, taking great care to be presentable, just like this man he greatly respected.

These moms had no idea how hurtful or uncaring their comments felt. Were people really that shallow? Couldn't they see past the un-tucked shirt and words in hand to the miracle happening in front of their eyes?

Despite this one breakthrough of which I was immensely proud, I still saw Sam's home schooling adventure as a mistake. After one semester we enrolled him at the school connected with our church. At the entrance interview, I made sure they understood Sam's needs, and explained that no matter how he did academically, I truly believed he was going to thrive at a Christian school.

Sam associated this school with God, and they needed to make sure he had passing grades, even if his work didn't show it. God did not fail people, so they could not fail Sam. I made sure they understood this before I signed the enrollment papers. I was not asking them to pass where he shouldn't pass, but I was making it clear that they needed to put the time and effort in to ensure he was capable of passing—because he could not believe that God had failed him. Not here.

He had an awesome teacher second semester of his third grade year. Mrs. Gibson had studied special education in graduate school, so she absolutely loved Sam and worked hard to make sure he succeeded. If he turned in a failing paper, she told him she must not have done a very good job explaining it to him. Then she took time to work with him until he got it right.

Mrs. Gibson blessed Sam daily. On more than one occasion, as I dropped him off at her classroom in the morning, she stepped out in the hall to give me a hug or pray with me. She knew the difficulty we had parenting Sam. She blessed me as well.

As Sam attended this school, I had the opportunity to start a band class for fourth thru sixth graders. I missed teaching music, and thought it might bring some joy back into my life. As Katie embraced her own band experiences, this felt like the perfect opportunity to return to my roots.

I set up a time with the music store to let kids try out instruments, and they provided rentals. I prayed ahead of time that God would give me a well-rounded group, because a band with five trumpets and three drums wouldn't work very well. He heard this prayer, and I started with 22 students and a totally balanced group.

We met twice a week, and started a more advanced group after one semester. Sam wanted to play, and I hoped we could find a way to connect through music. He picked the trumpet, and during our practices he got to see me as a successful band teacher.

I think it gave Sam an opportunity to see me in a different light. I caught him smiling when I made the kids laugh, or taught them something difficult and they succeeded. He could tell I cared about them and that they liked me in return. Sam and I enjoyed each other during band class.

Katie helped me with the younger players each week. She had played French horn for several years, and she also played the trumpet. She handled the entire brass section for me when I needed to work with the woodwinds or percussion. This was also gratifying for her, as it helped her to feel pride in the group and the ways in which she was able to act as a leader.

Sam struggled reading the music, relating the notes to the correct fingering, and finding the right pitch. Most of the kids picked it up quicker than he did, but he didn't seem to grow too frustrated. The second year, all of the kids moved up to the advanced band, but I kept Sam in the beginning band. His skill level simply wasn't at a place for advancement yet.

Because I kept him back, he became the leader of the trumpets in beginning band, and helped the newer players as they struggled with some of the things he had now mastered. He liked to be a leader, and experienced some of the same pride Katie had the year before. It turned out to be the best thing possible to have held him behind. He didn't seem to understand that he was "held back." He just saw himself as the one to help the new students.

I truly enjoyed this time with him. We had fun and respected each other, and we made beautiful (in the beginning band sort of way) music together.

Chapter Twenty-Eight

MY IDEA OF God, His character, how He loves and speaks, and what I believed about His heart toward me changed dramatically from our time in Vietnam and into the years that followed.

We attended church, not for our particular beliefs or convictions, but because Bob and I felt obligated. We were both raised in traditions that emphasize church attendance and religious activities. At the time Sam arrived, we attended church with my mom and her sister. Mom offered to attend one service, and then take Sam to Sunday School so that we could continue attending service ourselves. Because of his struggles, he couldn't go by himself back then, and we really needed a break during church. This loving act helped us immensely in those first few years.

Outside this church, I began attending a bible study with a Pampered Chef friend. From my youth, I had felt a longing for God.

I had accompanied some friends to an event sponsored by Campus Crusade for Christ during my senior year in high school, and had heard the story of Jesus in a way that touched my heart deeply and remained with me always. I felt an actual love for Him and understood how He had suffered for me. I changed at that event, but the church I attended didn't offer experiences to grow deeper in this kind of love relationship.

I attended a few bible studies at church, but left feeling there were no answers. We all read something from The Bible and sat around saying, "What do you think it meant?" "I don't know, what do you think it meant?"

I didn't see the point, and I didn't have time for that sort of thing when I was still young and unencumbered.

This new study I attended showed great promise. The teacher taught as if there actually *were* answers to be found in The Bible, unlike the previous studies I had attended. I began to understand God's character, and the stories from The Bible started to make sense. I saw The Bible as one story and how the parts fit together. I had never read a single book of The Bible straight through before. The women in this group helped me learn and process what we studied.

Over time, however, it started to seem that some of these people loved The Bible more than they loved God. They focused much energy on memorizing scripture and reciting it for rewards. I understand the value in knowing what God has to say about life, but it seemed like too much emphasis was placed on what The Bible said in black and white, instead of embracing a vibrant relationship with the living God who wrote that book. The few times I asked for guidance with difficult life situations, the pastors or teachers quoted directly from The Bible. They couldn't seem to develop their own thoughts based on the principles from The Bible. I desired to be around people who knew what The Bible said, and also trusted God to guide their thoughts and words individually. I needed to find a place with joy and grace. This perception of legalism began to feel like a burden, and I already had too many burdens.

We moved to a mega-church in town and found the grace our hearts longed for there. The music sounded like Christian radio, and the teaching was applicable.

The church we left had emphasized knowledge of scripture as the main goal for those seeking spiritual maturity. I learned a lot of scripture, and read much of The Bible. But I still hungered for more.

I needed God. I needed to know God now. My head knew the facts, stories, and how it all fit together, but my heart ached for intimacy with God. I had learned too many things that had actually hurt my relationship with God over the years—now I needed to rebuild that.

During a conversation with my bible study teacher, I told her I seriously needed to hear from God. I prayed daily and asked Him to speak to me. She read from Jeremiah 17:9: "The **heart** is deceitful above all things, and **desperately wicked**: Who can know it?" She told me that my first thought would be fleshly, so I should reject it. Because of my wicked heart, I would obviously think in opposite terms than God.

But my heart already belonged to God. When I gave it to Him, He gave me a new, clean heart. I prayed day after day asking for God's love, guidance, wisdom, and encouragement. He gave it to me daily, but upon the counsel of this teacher, I too often rejected it as my own thought. I waited for Him to correct my evil thinking, and ended up feeling like God wouldn't speak to me.

As my relationship with God grew organically rather than legalistically, I found myself needing to change some of my friendships. I discovered this awesome closeness to God that changed how I related to people. I wanted my friends to join me as I grew, but I think it scared them. We grew farther and farther apart, the distance between us consistently widening. I lost several friends in this process. These losses devastated me, but my relationship with God blossomed.

With the losses, my insomnia returned with a vengeance. I literally spent five months awake, sleeping no more than 10 hours total. I tried melatonin and every other sleep supplement available, alone and in combinations. I searched the Internet, tried over-the-counter sleep aids, took warm baths, exercised hard early in the day, ate right…and still stayed awake.

After the first few weeks, things happened that scared me. My eyes ached so much that I could hardly keep them open during the day. I stopped driving, cooking, and cleaning, and had a difficult time doing anything for my family.

Friends brought us meals and paid to have someone clean our house. Bob told me he struggled to come to terms with my disabling condition.

I went to church each week and hid in the back. I knew I would cry through the entire service. This went on for weeks. I always left immediately so I wouldn't run into people I knew. I was an absolute mess, and even though I thought church should be a safe place for messy people, it wasn't. Not my kind of messy, anyway.

One Sunday, a kind older man who taught a class Bob and I attended saw my suffering. I fell apart. I collapsed and found myself sobbing, telling him my troubles. He gave me the number of a Christian psychiatrist he had heard lecture at Denver Seminary.

I made an appointment truly believing the doctor would confirm my insanity. I didn't know anything about psychiatrists, except that they treated crazy people.

All my life, people had teased me about the depth of my emotions. At one point as a child, I had prayed that God would give me His emotions, so I could feel things the way He did. I wanted to know Him more, so I prayed to see things with His eyes. He answered that prayer. The Bible is full of stories of Jesus displaying his emotions to the full extent. When He felt joy, He expressed it greatly. When He was angry, people knew it. When He felt sad, He cried bitterly.

I feel deeply as well. This made some people nervous around me. I feared this doctor would diagnose me with some disorder or mental disease with a horrible social stigma. I dreaded being labeled as crazy, and now I had an appointment to meet the doctor who could confirm my insanity.

Instead, Dr. Larry Sanders treated me with such kindness and gentleness. I told him my fears of being crazy, and he reassured me that "crazy" isn't even a diagnosis. Whatever I was experiencing had treatment options available. I cried in relief. He wasn't scared of me or my deep emotional reservoir.

We talked about the pressure of raising a child with severe anxiety, and how Sam's nervousness made me anxious. My failure to fix my son and my family had cast me into a deep depression. I told him that having a diagnosis of depression was depressing, and we both laughed. The insomnia troubled him, as it did me. He started me on another anti-depressant, and later added an anti-anxiety medication. Both had side effects of drowsiness, but I still couldn't sleep. I certainly felt drowsy, though.

Dr. Sanders and I talked a lot. He worked hard to earn my trust, because he had been through his own hard times. He didn't see me as mentally unstable, but as someone living through a lot of trauma. He never judged me, but he challenged some of my thinking—about God, about me, about adoption, about parenting, and about how I was parented.

I journaled, believing God could see and hear my words, and that He cared for me deeply.

After trying a few medications for sleep, I felt like I was dying, and desperately needed to sleep. Fear had crept in and taken a strong hold on my heart. Dr. Sanders said he could put me in the hospital and medically induce a deep sleep, but we agreed that I was not dying, and God might want to use this time with me for a higher purpose.

After much trial and error, Dr. Sanders finally found a combination of medicines that made me fall asleep and stay asleep. I slept for the better part of a week. When I awoke and started to live again, I found I had learned some deep lessons through that horrible time.

In my journal, I wrote:

"LESSONS LEARNED WHILE NOT SLEEPING":

- *God is the only One I can depend on. He will never give up on me. He is the One to reassure me and tell me it will be okay. He never gets tired of me. He's always there.*

- *The sadness comes to the surface when I'm tired. I feel more intensely. I discovered the depths of the losses I'd experienced thus far.*

- *Outside things don't matter. I don't care what others think. I don't care what the house looks like. Nothing material matters, only what I can learn from my Lord. I devour bible study and devotions asking, "What will You tell me today? Give me something. Help me in some way. Speak to me!"*

- *Choose to do the right thing. Choose life. Live responsibly and humbly.*

- *Grief: At the end of the fight, when nothing works and nothing is left to try or do, there is profound sadness.*

- *Forgiveness: Remember the person in the good times. Choose to live in a merciful universe instead of a fair one. If I don't forgive, my kids won't forgive. I don't want to live as a victim, and I don't want the kids to either.*

- *Forgiving is costly. I must give up the right to get even. Let God run the universe, not me. Let God judge and show His mercy. Healing requires forgiveness, so I will forgive. Unforgiveness makes people sick. It is a process, not an event. Forgiveness cancels the consequences of the wrongdoing. I give up the right to punish them. I want to be the recipient and the extender of grace, love, and the healing power of God.*

- *Christ intercedes for me to the Father. He gives me power. He will fix this, or He will enable me to sustain.*

- *God is sovereign. He is bigger than my circumstances and He will make my life better through my circumstances.*

- *The Sovereign God came in Jesus Christ to suffer with me and to suffer for me. He descended deeper into the pit than I will ever know. His sovereignty did not protect Him from loss—it led Him to suffer loss for MY sake.*

- *He is vulnerable to pain. He weeps and is acquainted with grief. God is a suffering sovereign who feels the sorrows of the world. I bring my pain to God, but also feel the pain God suffered for me. He understands suffering because He suffered.*

- *I can't protect my children from suffering, but I can go through it with them.*

- *I need more than a temporary miracle. I need a resurrection to make life eternally new. All tears, pain, and sorrow will be swallowed up in everlasting life, and pure, inextinguishable joy.*

Chapter Twenty-Nine

*I*N THE SUMMER of 2007, when the kids were 15, 14, and 11, we took a camping trip to Yellowstone National Park. We planned the trip to last 10 days as we traveled through Grand Teton National Park. This trip was the ultimate expression of our earlier love for camping.

Over the years, Brendan and Katie had grown weary of Sam's attempts at controlling, manipulating, and annoying people.

I had been seeing a therapist, Mary Ellen, for several years. I spent a few weeks with her to prepare for this trip, so we could not just survive but hopefully enjoy some of it. Mary Ellen seemed to understand the strain we lived with on a constant basis. She understood Sam as well. Upon her advice, we arranged the car so that Sam could sit in the back by himself.

Katie and Brendan sat together in the middle seat with a DVD player to watch movies. Sam asked to watch, but he talked or made noise so that no one could hear the movie. We supplied him with plenty of car-friendly activities—books, stickers, clay, toys—all meant to provide him with personal entertainment. He didn't play with anything we gave him. He talked almost constantly instead.

We ignored him, per our counselor's advice.

The other kids used headphones to listen to their movies while Bob and I listened to books on tape or talked to each other. Once in awhile, I checked in with Sam to see how he was doing, and the nonsense started again—so we would tune him out.

Upon our arrival at the campground in Yellowstone, Sam needed to use the bathroom. We started setting up the camper, and saw the bathroom about 100 yards away. Brendan took him to the outhouse, turned him around to see our camper, and told him how to get back when he finished.

Several minutes went by, and we noticed Sam had not returned.

Brendan went to look for him, and couldn't find him. Panic set in. We had not familiarized ourselves with this huge campground yet. We all started shouting Sam's name. We yelled louder and louder as we looked from the bathroom to the camper and back again.

Other campers knew we were looking for a child and offered to help. We told them to look for an Asian boy with jeans and a red shirt. Pretty soon, many people were screaming his name and it felt like the whole campground had joined the search.

We searched for almost an hour before someone finally said that they had heard a campsite down the way had found a young boy. Hurrying down, we reunited with Sam about a mile from our campsite, eating with another family. He had walked out of the bathroom and headed the opposite direction of our campsite and just kept walking. He talked to lots of people on his solo venture and apparently wasn't afraid. I truly believe that with his attachment issues within our family, anyone could have taken him home and he would have gone without a fight.

We had fun the rest of the trip, but the thick tension and fights were plentiful. The highlight was a boat ride on a lake—Brendan and Katie taking turns driving, Sam getting a chance to drive while sitting on Bob's lap. The breeze felt so good, and the sound of the motor kept the conversation to a minimum.

Looking back, it's sad to think we did better as a family when we spent time together in silence.

At the end of one long hard day, Sam and I stayed in the camper to work through his poor attitude. Everyone else had left because of the tension. I talked to him, as I had hundreds of times before, about how to be a good friend to Katie and Brendan. I explained how his actions caused them to want to stay away from him, and what he could do to make things better. He seemed to understand, and said he did want to be friends with his brother and sister.

He didn't know why he did what he did. Frustrated, Sam screamed, "I don't fit in this family!"

As I had on many other occasions, I reassured him that I loved him and we would work at this as long as it took. He was a part of our family, and God didn't make mistakes.

As the words came out of my mouth though, my heart doubted. He wanted to be the oldest, but was the youngest. He loved sports, and we didn't enjoy sports with his passion. Brendan had a sarcastic sense of humor. Sam didn't understand normal humor, let alone the twisted humor of sarcasm. He asked so many annoying questions, no one in the family wanted to engage in conversation with him anymore.

He really *didn't* fit.

We had tried so hard for so many years to make it work, but it often seemed like trying to shove a round peg into a square hole.

No matter how hard we tried, it just wasn't working.

Chapter Thirty

AFTER THAT TRIP, it felt like one thing after another hit our family, starting with another surgery for Sam.

Sam had snored like crazy from the day we met, his nose almost too small for air to pass through. The orthodontist had commented on the size of his adenoids after looking at X-rays of his jaw. The adenoids blocked the air from moving between his nose and mouth, causing Sam to snore.

We already knew that he had an under bite, but the doctor informed us of its extreme nature. The doctor worried that if his lower jaw didn't grow to catch up, he would have to endure jaw surgery later in life. This would include breaking and resetting his jaw, then wiring it shut until it healed. That sounded like nothing but pure misery, and we couldn't imagine Sam in that much pain, having to drink his food through a straw. The orthodontist thought the lack of oxygen due to his enlarged adenoids and turbinates might be complicating things, and he suggested we take him to an ear, nose, and throat doctor.

Sam endured his fifth surgery. He asked me to call the church so the pastor would come pray with him before he went in. For a child who had been through many surgeries, this had become the usual protocol. Our new, larger church did not function this way though. Instead of sending the pastor Sam knew, they sent the pastor's father.

He was a lovely man of God, and I'm sure he meant well, but Sam didn't know him or want him in the room. He prayed quickly and left.

The doctor performed this surgery on the opening day of the new Children's Hospital in Denver. Despite the great facility, the surgery was an ordeal, and Sam felt horrible after his release. He threw up on the way home and begged me to stop the car. The driving made him sick to his stomach. The slow ride home felt like forever.

Sam stayed home from school for an entire week to recover. For such an active child, this was torture. He had a difficult time staying on the couch, and missed his friends. This child had endured more than most adults would in their entire lives, and again I was faced with the unfairness of this world.

Brendan continued to struggle in school. Geometry became his nemesis, a never-ending torture. After switching schools and getting tutored through fourth quarter, he found out he still had one more chapter to complete, on the final day of school. This did not go over well. His teacher gave him the opportunity to finish the last assignment and still receive credit for the class, but he wanted school to be finished and summer to begin.

I could see his anger during the car ride home. The last day of school was usually a day for celebrating, but this year we did not celebrate.

I understood, and wanted him to know it.

"I bet it doesn't feel very good to find out you have more to do, when you thought you were done."

"I'm so sorry it didn't work out the way you hoped."

"This is really a bummer, I get it."

It didn't matter. We arrived home, and Brendan opened his door with gusto. He didn't intend this to happen, but his door slammed into the post in the middle of the garage. If he had been able to calm himself, we would have dealt with this accident and moved on. But he didn't. On the rebound of his door slamming into the post, he forced it back into the post again, deliberately. He let out his anger, and it felt good. For a moment.

Sam's school still had one more week, but Katie waited for us at home. As we went into the house, she immediately hid behind me. She felt Brendan's anger and got scared. "I'm not doing it! You can't make me!" Brendan screamed and pounded his fists. I tried to calm him down, but nothing worked. I said, "Get in the car, Katie." We left Brendan at home.

We both cried and drove around. Brendan called on my cell phone several times, frantically trying to apologize. I didn't answer. I wanted him to sit with himself and feel the impact of his actions. I took the car to a repair shop and got an estimate for the work that would need to be done. Brendan needed to take responsibility for his actions, but he could not pay for the repairs.

After what seemed to be a long time, I finally answered my phone. I hated leaving him home alone like that, but knew he wouldn't learn if he didn't experience the consequences of his behavior. "I'm so sorry, Mom. I don't know why I did it," he pleaded. I told him about the estimate and that he needed to figure out how to pay for part of the damage. I also told him that his behavior had scared Katie and that we wanted reassurance he had calmed down before we came home. He told me he could stay calm.

Katie and I returned home. "We need to talk, Brendan." He tried to walk away. "You will listen, or I'll call the police. You may never scare Katie or me like that again. You have the choice to either see a counselor and deal with your anger, or face the police if you lose control again. Do you understand?" He agreed to see a counselor without hesitation.

He never lost control like that again, but started learning how to deal with his anger in a healthy way.

Sam wasn't even aware of this situation. It had nothing to do with him. And yet, the long-term effects of living with a child with Reactive Attachment Disorder continued to tear us apart as a family.

Chapter Thirty-One

As summer approached, I felt major anxiety. It became my constant companion. Sam didn't function well outside of the structure of school. I had always been a fairly organized person, but I didn't have the energy to schedule our summer in 15-minute increments. I remembered how much we had loved summer when the kids were little, but the last few years, we had simply been trying to survive.

I spent hours that spring searching the Internet for camps, programs, and anything else that might keep Sam busy and give the rest of us a break. As I spoke with the various programs, however, it became obvious that none were set up for a child like ours. His issues were greater than they could handle.

One of the problems I had grown increasingly concerned about was Sam's skin-picking. For years now, he had been picking at his skin obsessively throughout the day. He probably had 100 wounds in various stages of healing at any one time. As he approached puberty, I grew concerned that the picking would turn into cutting, so I took him to Dr. Sanders, who prescribed an anxiety-reducing beta-blocker medication.

I sat in on the initial appointment between the two of them. The doctor asked Sam questions like why did he pick? How did it make him feel? How long did the feeling last? How soon did he feel the need to pick again? When did he pick the most often? What happened when he tried not to pick?

The doctor stayed calm as he listened to Sam's answers, and I could tell he had dealt with much worse cases in the past. Sam's picking had become a huge problem. He looked like an abused child. I hated that he did this to himself, and that it seemed as though nothing we had tried helped. Starting the beta-blocker at least seemed like a step in the right direction.

I talked to the school nurse and told her about his new medicine, asking if she would watch out for any side effects. She called the first week. The medicine made Sam calm, but sleepy. He had fallen asleep in class several times. It affected his reflexes, and he wasn't doing as well in P.E. class as he previously had been. He loved playing basketball, but his slow reflexes now made it dangerous for him to play.

We adjusted the dosage a few times, and held back the dose when he had practice or a game after school. That helped a bit, but we still wanted to see more significant improvement.

After checking out a residential treatment facility for children with attachment issues, I started to realize how much I needed a break. I really wanted the treatment center to accept Sam for the summer. I thought he might get some much-needed help, and we might get some rest and be able to have fun without our increasing frustrations with Sam ruining it.

Even writing these words makes my heart hurt. I never wanted to feel that way about my son, but…it seemed as though our family had been struggling for an eternity, and that potentially removing him from the center of things could help to bring us back together. Our insurance would not cover the treatment. I offered to sell my car, or take out a loan to pay for it.

I kept looking at other options. I found out about a day psychiatric treatment program at The Children's Hospital in Denver, and started my research. Our insurance *would* cover this program.

After spending several hours talking to the intake people, having them consult with our psychiatrist, and filling out piles of paperwork, we made the decision to enter Sam into this program.

It started on his last day of school, so I had to pull him out early. I spoke with his teachers and principal and they all agreed that Sam would benefit from the program and that it was worth missing the last few hours of school. The hospital admitted Sam for 11 days of treatment. He attended Monday through Friday from 8:00a.m. until 3:00p.m.

His treatment plan listed several goals:

1. To stabilize his medications under the direction of their psychiatrist, by observing his behavior and monitoring his blood work.

2. To improve his behavior, stopping the scratching and picking.

3. To help improve his focus and work through emotional issues.

We committed to attend all parent and family therapy as directed by the team of staff members working on Sam's case.

I struggled to think about him going into this program, and at first even wondered if he needed this amount of care. My doubts soon faded, however, when the hospital requested seven additional days, and the insurance company approved without hesitation.

My child was in trouble.

I cried every day after I dropped him off. I was so sad to think that my son needed this amount of intensive psychiatric care. Some days, I stopped by to see my friend, Kelly, at her consignment store. She listened to me with great compassion and seemed to understand my pain.

Kelly and I had known each other through bible study for several years. She and her husband, Tom, had invited Bob and me to dinner once to talk about adoption. At the time, they had two boys and were looking into adopting a girl. They knew we had struggled with our adopted kids, and wanted to hear the reality of adoption—not just the fluffy good stuff most people hear. We told them they'd better make sure their marriage was in great shape, and have a counselor on hand for tough times. We suggested they read up on attachment issues, and make sure they had a great support system in place. I said, "Wounded children seem to know where you are weak, and they continually poke your buttons. The healthier you are emotionally, the better you'll be as parents."

As I spoke the words, I realized I must not be as healthy as I once thought, because Sam knew every one of my buttons.

They ended up not going through with their own adoption because Kelly found out she was pregnant...with twins!

Sam's stay at Children's brought us renewed hope that things would improve, and we worked hard to follow the medical and behavioral protocol set for us through the summer. Things seemed a little better, but the changes didn't necessarily feel deep, or real.

Somehow, I felt Sam did what they asked of him in order to get rewards or special games, or fun activities, but if they didn't offer a reward, he didn't care about true change.

I struggled with the treatment I received from the psychiatrists at Children's as well. They acted as if Sam's issues were new to me.

"When you pick him up, if you could hold his hands and look him in the eye while you talk about how things went in his session, it will build trust."

Did they really think I didn't know that, or hadn't been trying it for years? They tried to deal with Obsessive-Compulsive Disorder (OCD) and Generalized Anxiety Disorder (GAD), but they didn't understand how Reactive Attachment Disorder (RAD) played in. They recommended an extensive workup with a neuropsychologist, to determine how Sam's brain affected his behavior. After they discharged Sam from their program, we scheduled another six days worth of testing for a few thousand dollars.

The results of this testing showed Sam suffered from Reactive Attachment Disorder (RAD), Attention Deficit Hyperactivity Disorder (ADHD), Obsessive-Compulsive Disorder (OCD), Generalized Anxiety Disorder (GAD), Post Traumatic Stress Disorder (PTSD), and a new one—Non-Verbal Learning Disorder (NVLD).

What more could we learn? What more could we do?

I got my hands on as many books as I could, voraciously learning about Non-Verbal Learning Disorder so I could *train* Sam's special education teachers about his newest diagnosis.

Fall arrived and with it hopes of a good school year. He changed teachers, but the special education staff remained mostly intact. The year started out well, and everyone liked Sam.

Outside of our home, no one understood our problems. Sam was funny, charming, likable, friendly, helpful, outgoing. Everything he wasn't at home. We lived in a fairly small town, and each time we went out, we heard choruses of "Hi Sam!" Sometimes we didn't even know where Sam knew the people from, but they all knew him…and liked him…and most likely would never understand my overwhelming exhaustion and desperation about how to continue raising such a high-maintenance little guy who responded to everyone else far better than he responded to me, his own mother.

I felt even more isolated.

I had to constantly remind myself that this is typical RAD behavior—to refuse to bond with the primary caretaker following a lengthy early childhood in an orphanage. It wasn't that Sam couldn't connect with and love me. It was that Sam couldn't connect with his adoptive mother, and I *was* that adoptive mother. But this didn't lessen the burden…or alleviate the frustration…or sooth the isolation.

The more desperate I felt, the more I looked for support. If I couldn't find the help I needed, I tried to create it. I decided to find other adoptive moms struggling with their children. I knew I must not be the only mom out there suffering. I wanted to find women who understood the issues of attachment disorders. I also needed to find moms willing to continue this battle, no matter what.

I approached a few women about starting a group. Two expressed interest. One decided she couldn't be part of our group with the stipulation I had included—that we all be committed to continuing to parent, no matter what. This family had already decided they couldn't parent their child because she had threatened to kill them. They were in the process of deciding what to do next, looking for a family who may be willing to take her—one more capable of handling these major issues. This family had adopted from the same orphanage we did. We had met their daughter in Vietnam, and again in Colorado. We *knew* these people. What must they be going through to consider relinquishing their daughter?

I had never considered choosing another family for my own child.

This other woman's decision scared me, because it brought up thoughts I tried to prevent from surfacing. Her family had come to a conclusion that terrified me. I didn't even want to consider it. It felt like torture as I listened to her describe the search for her daughter's new parents. It didn't seem right. How could someone do this?

And what if my family had to?

Chapter Thirty-Two

*I*NEVER HID OUR struggles with Sam, with our marriage, or with our family dynamics from our friends, extended family, or church leadership. I asked for help anywhere and everywhere I could. I spoke openly about our problems, because my desperation trumped my pride. I remember thinking I would crawl up the aisle of our church on my hands and knees if it would help. I had no problem asking those I thought might have answers or resources for help.

Our entire family had been suffering from exhaustion as a result of dealing with Sam; I went to several pastors, leaders, elders, and others in positions of authority at our church. At the time, attendance at our church averaged about four thousand people per weekend. I figured that with numbers like those, somebody had to know a way for us to get help.

I asked for names of empty nesters that might like to spend time with a pre-teen who loved to watch sports. Maybe their grandchildren lived far away, and Sam could be a surrogate grandson.

I asked if there were any college-age boys who might be interested in becoming youth pastors, or coaches. Would someone like to mentor this child and play basketball with him—maybe take him to McDonald's here and there? We would pay for both of them, of course. We just needed someone else Sam could look up to—someone who could take on a few extra hours a week with him, providing us relief from the constant day-to-day struggles of parenting him.

We knew a family with many children. The mom offered to watch Sam at their home a few times, and he fit in great! There were kids everywhere, so if he bothered someone, he could move on to someone else. They were so kind and loving to Sam and to me. The mother seemed to understand our situation, and had actually been looking for this kind of opportunity. I felt such relief on the days Sam went to their house after school. My anxiety calmed for a few hours, and I knew he was safe and having fun. This lasted for several weeks and helped tremendously, but soon scheduling issues and some commitments on their part caused the arrangement to end.

We tried to find another family willing to help, but couldn't. So many people seemed to have an opinion on our situation, but so few seemed willing to help. I knew no one truly realized our level of desperation, but by this point, we had been parenting Sam for seven years. It was only getting harder. Not easier.

It seemed the attitude of many people was, *You decided to adopt. He's your kid, so deal with him.*

I went to some of the male pastors at church and spilled my heart. I told them my husband needed male friends to walk alongside him, and begged them to reach out. I didn't feel as if anyone truly made an effort, although one pastor did leave Bob a message on his phone. Bob knew he could go to the men's group at church, but his life was imploding. He needed to be able to share what was going on in a vulnerable way, but not through the structure of a large group. Things were reaching a boiling point at home. All of our kids seemed to be suffering, and we weren't connecting as a couple. This situation was literally tearing us apart from the inside out. People didn't understand that. We felt out of place and unsupported.

Maybe if it had all fallen apart shortly after bringing Sam home, people would have at least been able to comprehend it. But this had been a slow burn, building up steadily over the years. We loved Sam. We wanted to help him, but the situation was eating away at us, chipping at our sanity and ability to even support each other. So many times, I felt like we would fall apart. But we always found a way to keep moving forward, slapping masking tape on the cracks and continuing to push.

That was what we were supposed to do.

It wasn't acceptable to admit defeat.

To admit that while you loved your child, that love was destroying you. Even though I hadn't yet found help, I continued to ask.

I shared the deteriorating condition of our family with our pastor. About a week later, we went out to eat after church. The pastor and his family sat at the booth right next to us, and said nothing. I knew he saw us, but he pretended he didn't. It shocked me. I didn't understand how he could preach all morning, and then an hour later ignore the people he had just preached to? Perhaps he was just "respecting our time and space," but at the time it felt like we were simply "too much" for him to handle.

We had tried to befriend another couple that had adopted several children. We supported them and even met them at the airport to welcome their new children home. Once again, I had Sam with me at a restaurant a few months later, and the mother and her daughters stood directly in front of us to order. Sam asked if we could sit with them, but the mom ignored us. Again, they sat one table away, unreachable.

Maybe they were afraid. Perhaps as parents of newly adopted children, we scared them in the same way the woman choosing a new family for her daughter had scared me. Maybe our situation was too heavy for them, when they were in the midst of trying to build their own family. Maybe they were totally focused on something else, and didn't even see or hear us.

But Sam felt rejected. So did I.

I spoke with a different pastor several times at church, on the phone, and during prayer time. He knew our situation: We were losing the battle to help our son, our marriage was falling apart, and our children were suffering. He suggested we take it to our small group. We had done just that, but some of the members felt overwhelmed by the enormity of our situation, and our group fell apart. The group members told us to take it to the pastor, and the pastor told us to take it to our small group.

Help! I'm drowning here!
I don't know where else to go!
Is there anybody out there?
Can anyone hear me?

Chapter Thirty-Three

O VER THANKSGIVING BREAK, we took a trip to Disney World. Planning for it brought back wonderful memories of the trip we had taken as a family of four before Sam joined us. I had no idea that this would be our last trip as a family of five...

Excitement filled our home as preparation took over. We anticipated and planned all the places to visit well in advance. We'd traded our time-share for a great place in Orlando, so we knew we had fabulous accommodations waiting for us.

The familiar issues started immediately.

As soon as we checked into our accommodations, the questions began in rapid-fire succession: "Where are we going first? What time? Can we go now? Why do we have to sleep? I'm not tired." Sam woke up at 6:00 Florida time, which felt like 3:00 to the rest of us. The two teenagers did not want to wake up this early. This was their vacation.

To let the rest of us sleep awhile longer, Bob took Sam out for coffee and donuts.

At about 10:00, we headed out to our first park—Sea World. We went straight to the Shamu show, and arrived in time to sit just behind the splash zone. As soon as the show started, Sam looked straight at me, yawned as big as I had ever seen him yawn, and lay down to fall asleep.

He would not watch the show.

Everything he had looked forward to had arrived, and he chose to sleep through it. If I hadn't seen this hundreds of times, I would have thought he was tired from getting up so early. I knew better. Through the years I had talked to him about this.

"Why do you sometimes fall asleep when we get to do something you really want to do?"

"Because I'm mad."

"But why don't you want to enjoy the fun?"

"Because I don't want to have fun with you."

"Do you want me to feel sad?"

"Sometimes."

He wanted to show us all that he would not enjoy anything we did that week. If we enjoyed it, he would act like he didn't care and chose not to participate. If something bored us, he enjoyed it thoroughly.

As we left Sea World, Brendan reminded me about Thanksgiving. I knew the date, but thought everyone wanted to spend Thanksgiving visiting the parks and eating fun food instead of doing the turkey dinner thing. It was only then, as he expressed his discontent, that I learned the importance Brendan placed on a turkey dinner with all the traditional side dishes.

We stopped by the only grocery store we had seen since our arrival the night before and put together our best Thanksgiving dinner: sliced turkey, canned gravy, instant mashed potatoes, green beans, stove-top stuffing, and three flavors of pie. It tasted pretty good, considering the last-minute shopping and our lack of energy for preparation.

Something in our delicious meal didn't agree with me though, and I got sick in the middle of the night. I couldn't remember the last time I had felt so sick. I vomited until there was nothing left, my head cradling the bathroom throne. Here we were at the "Happiest Place on Earth," and my face hugged a toilet for 24 solid hours.

Bob, Brendan, and Katie wanted to go to Universal Studios. They felt bad about leaving me, but the thought of the rides made me more nauseous. I didn't want them to miss out. Sam didn't want to go. I told him I couldn't take care of him, or spend time with him. I just wanted to sleep. He stayed in the main room of the condo and watched sports on TV all day.

My brain could not comprehend why he would come to Orlando and choose not go to Universal Studios.

Why would he sit in a hotel on vacation and stare at a television watching everything from swimming to women's college basketball?

I didn't care. I slept and threw up all day.

We found one benefit of going to the parks with Sam. His anxiety spiked from standing in long lines. He poked at people, screamed, and tried to sit down each time the line moved. After waiting for 45 minutes, we would have to leave the ride because Sam refused to go. Friends with the same kind of issue told us to speak with customer service when we arrived at Disney to explain our situation. We did, and they treated us with such dignity and respect. They gave all five of us passes to go to the front of the Fast Pass line, without checking in first. They dealt with all kinds of disabilities, and knew how frustrating it was for people to travel long distances and not be able to enjoy the parks.

Because of this pass, Katie and Brendan were able to enjoy the rides as many times as they wanted without having to wait in line. Sometimes Sam rode and sometimes he didn't, but either way, the rest of us got to enjoy the parks.

As we walked through Animal Kingdom, I held Sam's hand but he pushed me away. Later, he took my hand, but when he remembered he didn't want to love me, he jerked it back and gave me a horrible look—like he was mad at me for allowing him to forget he didn't love me.

His behavior caused stress in the rest of us. We fought over stupid things because of the high level of tension. After waiting for this trip for so long, we all wanted it to be over so that we could just go home. At least at home the kids could retreat to their rooms and escape the craziness that had become our lives.

We had not been on a vacation we enjoyed in seven years. Brendan and Katie were growing up, and I really feared they would leave our home as soon as they were able and never look back.

What were the consequences of all of this craziness on them?
What could I do, that I hadn't already done?

We had seen every doctor, therapist, counselor, specialist, psychologist, and teacher we knew existed. We'd taken Sam to clinics, vision therapy, occupational therapy, speech therapy, physical therapy, counseling, and hospitals. We had tried medication, behavior modification, group therapy, special education, respite and attachment therapy.

Insurance wouldn't pay for a residential treatment facility.

The elders at our church prayed over Sam. We prayed for spiritual, emotional, mental, and physical healing. I prayed over and over that God would heal Sam so he would feel like he belonged in our family. His words from our trip to Yellowstone remained forever in my head: "I don't fit in this family!"

Why did God have us travel all the way to Vietnam, spend eight years seeking every treatment available, spend thousands of dollars, not to mention all that time and energy loving him with everything we had, only to not heal him in the end?

Why would we go through all of this, only to feel like we were losing this battle, and with it our son and possibly our other children as well?

What was happening? I had tried with everything I had to give.

Why were things not working out for the best?

Chapter Thirty-Four

WE HOSTED A Christmas party for family and friends. Sam helped me decorate sugar cookies, and I watched his anxiety spike the closer it got to party time. He ran around the house in excitement, as he always did before a fun event. Around and around, from the living room, through the kitchen, past the dining room, and back through the living room he went. As the guests arrived, he found a spot on the floor and fell asleep.

We enjoyed having friends to our home. Our consistent turmoil had led us to isolate ourselves through the years. I didn't want Sam running through other people's homes, and it was hard to gather the energy needed to invite people to ours. But it was Christmas, and I wanted to create a good memory for our family. Our friends, Kelly and Tom, came to the party. Before they left, Kelly and I set up a lunch date in February to have some girl time.

Christmas morning, the kids awoke with excitement as usual. We gave Sam a snowboard. He looked at it, and put it in his room. I made the kind of cinnamon rolls that everyone loved. Sam wouldn't eat one, because I handed it to him. We stayed in our PJ's most of the day, but decided to put on clothes for our fancy Christmas dinner. Sam pulled his dirtiest clothes out of the hamper. After dinner, we watched a movie, but Sam refused to watch. He sang, blocked Katie's view, danced, and acted silly. Once again, we told him he needed to sit and watch, or go to the stairs. The battles didn't take a holiday.

On the last Friday before school started that January, I lay in bed crying. Vacations from the routine of school were always so difficult, and Sam had been home for two weeks now. It was too much. Even with the aid of anti-anxiety medication, I felt like I might have a heart attack, and I thought about how young my dad had been when he had died. Living under the constant strain of stares, conflict, anxiety, depression, and sleeplessness had taken its toll.

"I'm exhausted," I sobbed to Bob. "I can't do this anymore. I don't know what that means. I'm so scared. I truly think I'm going to die. If something major doesn't change, I'm not going to make it. My nerves are shot. I can't sleep. I can't take care of our home. I feel like we're losing Brendan and Katie. I'm so scared. Please believe me when I say you are going to end up being a single dad. I can't do this anymore. Please help me. Please help me."

Bob finally heard my heart. He understood I wasn't exaggerating and something had to change. I didn't know what needed to happen; I just knew it had to be something drastic.

We could *not* keep living like this.

After we talked, relief flowed through me like I hadn't felt in a long time. The future remained totally uncertain, but Bob had finally heard me. He held me as I drifted into a fitful sleep.

In the morning, I felt lighter. Just knowing that Bob was on board with me lifted a huge weight off my shoulders. His company always holds their Christmas party in January, and I needed to find something to wear. I didn't attend formal gatherings in those days, and I didn't have disposable income for a party dress.

We decided to stop at my friend Kelly's consignment store. As soon as we walked in the door, she said, "Guess what we're getting ready to do?"

"What?" we asked.

"We're getting ready to adopt."

As I remember back to that day in her store, Bob and I were surprised they were ready to adopt, so soon after having twins. Their older boys were nine and four, and the twins were one and a half. Their hearts must have really been set on adoption to want to pursue this path now. I immediately asked if they were going to Guatemala to get their little girl.

"No, God's made it clear that he's a boy...he's local...and he's older."

Bob and I just looked at each other. She smiled. "You got one you want to wrap up?"

Who asks that kind of a question?
This type of thing doesn't happen!
"Maybe," I found myself saying.

I couldn't even think. *What was she saying? I can't breathe. This isn't what I was talking about.* I just needed a break from exhaustion. She asked whether I was talking about the older boy or the younger boy. "Younger." I hung my head in shame. She had been a bit playful until that point—initially joking, until she saw the look on my face.

Now she wanted to know how she could help. She asked if they could take Sam the next day, Sunday, just to give us a break. She was the first person to see our desperation, and realize we were on the verge of breaking down. I felt a wave of gratitude. We immediately accepted her offer, and the next, when she invited him to come over the following weekend, from Friday after school through Sunday at bedtime. The thought of a weekend with just Brendan and Katie sounded like heaven. I truly hoped it would bring rest, and renewed energy to keep going. *Maybe Kelly and Tom could provide some respite to our family, and we'd be okay after all.*

Relief washed over me, even at just this small gift of precious time.

I knew Sam would have fun, be safe and welcomed. I desperately needed this. We *all* needed this. But the time passed so quickly, and my nerves didn't have a chance to calm down in between. Before I knew it, Sunday was over, and Sam returned home, his behavior worse than ever, and my nerves thoroughly on edge.

The following weekend, Sam packed a bag for his two-night sleepover. I slept in Saturday morning and truly crashed. We watched a few movies, but didn't have energy to engage in anything else. I worried about Sam. *How was he doing? Where did he sleep? Did he get along with their kids? Would he cause problems at their house*?

As planned, Sam returned at bedtime Sunday evening. Tom said they'd had a great weekend, but as he closed the door, Sam scowled at us and slammed his bedroom door.

I knew he must have been scared and anxious. He'd had fun and enjoyed his time at their house, but when he returned home, all emotions became exaggerated. He disobeyed more, scratched more, and manipulated more. Everything negative got worse.

He spent another weekend with Kelly and Tom, only to return with increasingly negative behavior.

He consistently did well with them, but then would always go into a tailspin with us.

Bob and I had dinner with Tom and Kelly, to talk about how we felt and what we wanted to happen. We all agreed to do what was best for Sam. What were the options?

Maybe he could spend weekends with them and come home during the week. So far, it seemed this pattern created more anxiety, and his behavior got worse at home.

Maybe he could stay with them for several months, giving us time to rest. We'd need to figure out how to approach this with him, and then transition him back.

How would he handle each scenario? We truly didn't know what the outcome of this would be. They were open to whatever we needed.

They also expressed their desire not just to babysit Sam, but to *adopt him.*

Mary Ellen truly got me through this season of my life. She knew about RAD, and the impact it has on families, especially the mothers. She had been with me as my health and my family deteriorated. We talked about Sam's behavior, my exhaustion, and the option presenting itself now. Our discussions led to Sam's severe attachment and learning issues, and how his brain didn't process the way mine did.

I had such great empathy and couldn't stand the thought of him feeling abandoned again. She reminded me that because of his Non-Verbal Learning Disorder, which is a frontal lobe brain injury, he lived in the moment. When he spent time with their family, he didn't sit around thinking about *us.* In many ways, this disorder may be a blessing in disguise in his life. Sam would not process feeling rejected over and over in his mind. He only focused on the present.

He enjoyed his time with them. When he came home, his anxiety came roaring out of his body like a tsunami.

Mary Ellen reminded me that my role in his life had always been to take all of his anger, fear, rage, anxiety, and every other negative emotion. He needed to dump it on someone, and it had been my role to take it. I felt I had been able to do THAT job. I didn't feel I had mothered or loved him well enough, but he had dumped all of his negatives emotions on me. It had always been a sort of love-hate relationship. I knew Sam loved me, to the extent that he could, but the trauma from his past prevented him from being able to trust me or connect with me. I knew I loved him with everything I had, but I couldn't find a way to help him bond with me.

I sobbed. I wanted to love my son and have him love me in return. But what if my role had been simply to receive all his hurt, so that he could get it out and move on with his life?

What if he could never heal in *our* home?

What if he *needed* a different family to have any chance of real attachment?

What if he needed me *out* of his life so he could truly thrive?

At that point, she asked me to stop thinking about what it would sound like, what other people would say, what my family would think, and just answer her question:

"What do *you* want to do?"

I couldn't answer.

I knew, but I couldn't say it.

I felt as if Sam was on a freight train barreling down the tracks, and I ran alongside trying to make sure he was okay. I could hardly run, and knew I couldn't keep going, but I couldn't stop until the train came to a station where someone waited for Sam.

The clock ticked. My insides screamed. Tears rained. Finally I whispered, "I want them to adopt him."

Bob asked about my session. It tore him apart. I realized I had been grieving my son for a few years. Bob couldn't comprehend our reality. He didn't want to believe what he knew to be true. We were losing our son. Our plan had never been to remove Sam from our family. We prayed and struggled, and prayed more, and struggled more.

He did not want to abandon his son.

This was the worst outcome Bob could have ever hoped for, and he felt like he had to choose between his wife and his son. If Sam stayed, he might lose me. If he stood up for me, he'd lose Sam. Bob suggested we rent an apartment. He would live with Sam, while Brendan, Katie, and I stayed in the house. We wouldn't be together as a family, but we could see each other sometimes. I couldn't live with that option. It wouldn't be fair to Brendan and Katie to lose their father.

At the same time, Brendan fought when we called him for dinner. The craziness wore him down, and he didn't even want to eat with us. He and Katie both used their rooms to escape more and more. I truly felt that if something didn't change soon, our family would not recover.

Sam spent several weekends with Kelly and Tom as Bob and I struggled. We felt relief from having him gone, but we still wished he could somehow just get better and stay in our family.

We prayed specifically for God to show us if Sam would be okay if this happened. He had never asked to go to their house, but he never objected. "Do you enjoy your time with their family?"

"Yep."

"What do you do?"

"Fun stuff."

"Do you ever feel scared?"

"No."

One Friday night, Bob took Sam to his basketball game without me. Kelly showed up with her boys to watch the game. Bob heard her oldest son talking with another boy during the game. The friend asked why he came. "To watch Sam," he said. The boy asked why, and he responded that Sam was going to live with them; they were going to be brothers.

Kelly later shared a conversation she'd overheard outside her oldest son's bedroom, when the boys were in bunk beds.

"Hey Sam? Wouldn't it be cool if we were brothers?"

"Yeah, man. It would be awesome!"

"We could have sleepovers every night!"

Sam had been to their house four times. We sat down as a family for dinner in the middle of the week. Out of the blue, Sam asked, "Can I go to their house this weekend?" Bob and I looked at each other and remembered our prayer from a few days earlier. We knew he must be somewhat conflicted, but he seemed to be slowly moving into their family.

The next week, Kelly and I sat in a restaurant for a lunch date that had been scheduled since December, before any of this craziness started. We talked about all the other members of our families, our jobs, and our lives. Finally, in the exact words of Mary Ellen, Kelly asked, "What do *you* want to do?"

I wept for several minutes before I was finally able to say, "We want you to adopt Sam."

She said, "Good, because that's what we want, too." Their family was ready.

One Friday after school, Sam decided he didn't want to go to Kelly and Tom's for the weekend. "Why are you making me go?" "I'm not packing and you can't make me!" "I don't want to go!" "Why do you do fun things with Brendan and Katie, and not me?"

"What do you mean, Sam?" I asked. It became apparent he didn't really believe that, but wanted to argue about something.

"Sam, do you remember our trip to Disney World? We planned that trip for all of us as a family. After we planned, waited, and finally got there, you refused to do anything with us.

"What do you want to do with Mom, Dad, Brendan, and Katie if you stay?" Sam thought for a minute, and then said he wanted to play with a friend down the street. I repeated, "What do you want to do with Mom, Dad, Brendan, and Katie?" He cried and couldn't think of anything.

"Can I hold you?"

I lay on the couch holding my son, and we both cried. He cuddled with me and we cried some more. I stroked his back and smelled his hair. Our tears joined together as they fell to the floor. For the first time, he didn't fight me. He relaxed into my arms and let me hold him tightly. *Why couldn't it always be this way?* For the first time, we connected over our breaking hearts. *Was this what it took?*

We snuggled for half an hour, when he suddenly jumped up and said he was ready to go. I held back my tears as I helped him pack. His mood totally changed. Happy, packed, and ready, he couldn't wait to leave.

I never held my son again.

The weekend of President's Day, Sam went to Tom and Kelly's house. Sunday evening Katie had a driving class. Her instructions for the evening driving session took her through our neighborhood. Katie told her teacher they were close to her house, so they came by to show off her new driving skills. She rang the doorbell, and I had a panic attack.

I thought Kelly and Tom had decided they couldn't handle Sam and were bringing him home. My heart started to race and my breathing increased.

I answered the door and tried to show Katie my pride with her driving. I almost collapsed as I closed the door. I literally couldn't breathe and my heart beat out of my chest. Bob stood by me. "I need to talk to you," I said.

He knew what I had to say before I said it. I cried from the depths of my soul. "I haven't even had a chance to let down, and Sam will be home tomorrow. I can't do it anymore. Will you call Kelly and Tom to see if he can stay longer?"

They said he could... stay... *forever.*

Sam needed more clothes. Tom drove him to school on Tuesday after the holiday, and wanted to pick him up and bring him to our house after school. Sam begged to walk home from school so his friends couldn't see him get into Tom's car and then ask questions. He walked home as if nothing had changed.

He arrived before Tom. I met him at the door and he fell apart; he was angry, sad, and confused. He started to cry. "I don't want to go! Why are you kicking me out of the house?"

"I'm so sorry this is so hard for you, Sam. I know you're sad and scared. I am too." Tom arrived with his oldest son, only to hear Sam say he didn't want to go to their house.

Sam sat on the stairs. "You can't make me go!" Tom and his son stood back in awkward silence, clearly feeling like intruders. Time passed slowly. "Stay away from me," Sam said angrily in my direction. I told Tom that Sam lived in the moment and would be okay once they all left together. I put some of Sam's things into his bag while he cried on the stairs. I guided my son out the door.

I watched Tom buckle *my* son into *his* car.

I thought back to the scene in the hospital after Brendan's birth and in some ways, this felt similar. Lisa had given her son to us, feeling pain mixed with relief. Just as she'd watched us buckle Brendan into our car, she'd wanted to make sure he was safe before she could let go.

Sam was safe. I could stop.

I haven't seen or spoken with my son since. At first we believed it might be easier to have him go gradually, but as time passed, we realized he needed to make the move and get out of limbo. The constant moving back and forth kept Sam in a state of intense anxiety. He needed stability in the midst of this major life transition.

I took Katie to All State Band two weeks later, and Sam returned home for the weekend. He and Bob had some time together, but Bob was in shock over the situation and spent the time simply trying to occupy Sam. He clearly didn't fit anymore.

Sam never came home again.

Chapter Thirty-Five

THE FIRST FRIDAY night after Sam was gone, we decided to get out of the house and do something. We had been in survival mode for so long, we weren't sure we knew how to live as a family anymore. We had dinner at a restaurant, and when the waiter asked, "How many in your party?" I responded, "Five, uh four."

He sat us at a table for five anyway. We experienced a strange combination of mourning, sadness, awkwardness, relief, and joy—all at the same time.

What happened next reminded me of the saying, "Sometimes you have to laugh to keep from crying." That's exactly what we did. We tried to tell jokes…make snarky comments about others in the restaurant…make rude noises just to get one another's attention. We tried to enjoy being a normal family.

Of course, we certainly did not feel like a normal family for years to come. But on this night, we tried to simply live in the moment (as Sam does), and it was a relief to relax and have a little fun.

Bob continued to visit with Sam weekly. Sometimes Sam cried and asked why he couldn't come home. Bob always assured him about our love for him and reminded him we wanted him to be happy. He told Bob he felt less anxious with his new family than with us. Bob sensed he felt badly about this, but Sam knew it was true. He called Kelly and Tom "mom and dad" when at their house.

The rest of us continued to struggle. We didn't automatically become a healthy, functioning family with Sam gone. Bob and I had problems in our marriage because we grieved so differently. Kelly and Tom struggled with the transition—who wouldn't? Sam had to make many adjustments. I suffered from horrible depression. Brendan and Katie didn't know how to talk about losing their brother with their friends or teachers. They both worried about other kids alienating them or teasing them. They suffered in silence.

As spring passed, my depression deepened.

I sat in the car with Bob as he spoke with Sam on the phone. I heard our little boy using better English than I had ever heard. For the first time in his life, he sounded like other kids his age. Dr. Fuller said he hadn't wanted to expend the energy to speak correctly with us. When he was in the presence of others, his language was near perfect. "Does he want to talk to me?" I whispered loud enough for Sam to hear.

"Um, uhh." I heard the struggle in his voice.

Sam clearly didn't want to talk to me. "Never mind," I mouthed to Bob. He told Sam he could do it another time.

I started the deep realization that for Sam to make it in life, I needed to be out of his world.

If we wanted him to attach to his new family, we couldn't keep pulling him back. I just wanted to be his mom—to help him grow, learn to love, and be happy.

I knew this was impossible in our home, with *me* as his mother. He would make it in life. He would indeed learn to love, grow, and be happy, but not with me in his life.

I had to let him go.

As this realization sunk in, I experienced a depression so deep that I stayed in bed for a week.

Bob and I had dinner with Tom and Kelly after Sam had been with them for several weeks. He seemed to function well with them, and they wanted to take him skiing over spring break. Snow sports are inherently dangerous. If Sam got injured while in their supervision, they needed to have the ability to make decisions on his behalf regarding his care. This caused us to sign over power of attorney so they could provide him with medical treatment if necessary. We knew we needed to do this, but it felt horrible.

Bob contacted a lawyer in Colorado Springs who specialized in this kind of work. The four of us met with him together in March. Bob and I arrived about 45 minutes before Tom and Kelly, which gave us time to talk to the attorney privately.

The attorney had handled many cases like this, and told me he saw the tremendous toll it took on the mothers in particular. He wanted me to know that he saw me as a loving, wonderful mother. He said he saw many children failing to thrive in their homes, but the parents couldn't deal with the thought of changing the situation. These children stayed in their homes, but couldn't ever get better.

We were giving Sam a chance to get better.

His words helped me tremendously. Up to this point, I had felt so judged by other people. He said things my heart needed to hear, making the reason for our meeting with him a bit easier. We signed over rights for Kelly and Tom to be able to provide anything Sam might need while in their care.

Part of me died inside.

Spring break approached quickly, and I asked Bob if we could do something as a family. Brendan and Katie had always wanted to bring friends on a vacation. We had purchased a time-share a few years earlier, and we were eager to exchange it for a week in Puerto Vallarta. The kids brought friends and had a great time. Bob and I rested and enjoyed watching the kids. We grieved over our missing son. We knew he would have hated this trip, but we still missed him.

Bob continued to struggle with the idea of Kelly and Tom adopting Sam. We knew it needed to happen. Knowing was not the same as doing. We finally spoke with the lawyer and started the long process of relinquishing Sam into Tom and Kelly's family.

During this process, Sam turned 12. This is the age when children are allowed to have representation in adoption proceedings. By the age of 12, the law states that children have a good sense of where they feel safe, and they should have a voice in deciding their fate. A social worker interviewed Sam about his feelings. He said he loved us, but felt less anxious with Tom and Kelly. The same social worker interviewed us for three hours. It was painful, but she validated that rarely did she see parents willing to do what was in the best interest of their children, especially if things weren't working.

The adoption moved forward slowly.

I paced the floor in my kitchen early on Easter morning, before my family awoke. I pleaded with God, my heart breaking. I knew I could not parent Sam with his attachment issues, but I never wanted to lose him.

"Why is this happening?"

"This isn't what I wanted!"

"My heart is breaking, and You could have prevented it!"

"Do You hear me?"

"Are You there?"

"Why did You have us go all the way to Vietnam, only to move him to another family?"

"Are You really asking me to give up my son?"

As I asked this final question, I remembered the date—Easter. I felt the familiar shame and guilt that usually accompanied my former beliefs about God. I expected God to blast me.

My beliefs had been changing for many years, and I knew the voice of God inside my heart. He didn't shame or condemn me. Instead, I felt Him whisper, "It really hurts, doesn't it?"

I collapsed to the floor. I realized He empathized with my pain.

In fact, God had given up His son, too.

He *knew* the pain of my loss.

He *knew* my grief, the absolute horror of this decision.

He didn't resent me for my pain, or scold me for expressing it.

He cared. He understood in a way no one else could.

I felt as if I had entered a place very few people ever experience. I understood a tiny bit of what God the Father experienced when He had to give up His Son—*all for my sake.*

I'd never felt closer to God than in that moment.

The remainder of the school year caused grief over strange things.

Sometimes Kelly didn't get Sam to school on time, or kept him home due to illness. The school would call me to find out why. I hated how awkward I felt having to explain our situation. The same thing happened when our many doctors, orthodontists, audiologists, and vision and dental offices called to confirm or set appointments.

At one point, I sent a generic letter to as many of Sam's old medical offices as I could think of, explaining the power of attorney and giving them Kelly and Tom's information.

Teaching band became very difficult for me, because Sam didn't come and the kids asked about him every week. They were too young to understand issues that even adults struggled to understand. How could I explain and not look like a monster to these children? The parents didn't ask, at first.

After several weeks, I told the students that Sam would not return. I explained that each of them had things they talked about as a family, but didn't necessarily share with other people. Our family had to deal with this and they didn't need to be burdened with it. I asked if they would please stop asking me about Sam, and simply pray for all of us. They respected that, and didn't ask anymore.

I told a few parents who asked me privately. I knew they were concerned for me, because I'd lost some weight and called a substitute a few times. I tried to stay focused on music, but everyone wanted to know about Sam. Some of them understood the devastation we had endured. They had compassion for our situation. Others seemed stunned and didn't know what to say. They picked up their children quickly and left without a word.

I became used to these responses.

As time went on, I realized that, for many adoptive families, I represented betrayal. "Please understand," I wanted to shout. "I love adoption! I'm all for adoption. Please don't shun me!" Many saw me as going against their cause, and they stopped trusting or even speaking to me. Most of them knew but probably forgot that we had adopted Brendan. He was still my son, and doing well.

Bob and I had not abandoned the cause of adoption. Our family was not the enemy. We were just broken, hurting people who needed love and compassion to make it through the loss of our son. We certainly did not need to be cast out and rejected. We were not the heartless monsters that some perceived us to be. We simply had to do what was best for our son, even if it was the most painful decision a parent could ever have to make.

One of my greatest sorrows came in a phone call. My old friend asked, "What happened with Sam?" She had just heard the news via the gossip train, and called to "hear my side of the story."

"What other side is there?" I asked. Two families got together to decide how to best help a struggling child. There was no other side.

She wanted me to show her where in The Bible God says it is okay to give up your child. I found this ironic, because at the start of our call, she had told me about a bible study she was doing focusing on Moses' mother—a woman who sent her infant down the Nile river in a basket hoping to give him a better life.

That fall, I cleaned Sam's room. I lovingly packed up the rest of his clothing and toys, anything he might like, hoping he might one day want something we had given him. I didn't want to throw anything away, but wanted Sam to have the choice of what to keep.

He didn't want anything I bought for him. He asked Kelly to buy him all new clothes, and he threw away his toys. That great new snowboard we gave him for Christmas? He never used it, and told Kelly he didn't want it.

I hated giving away Sam's bed. We had picked it out just for him. It had built-in dresser drawers under the bed because Sam hated using a dresser. I remembered helping him pick out his bedding, the paint, and the wallpaper for the room he only slept in for 10 months. Now the room was as empty as our hearts.

I found myself in a strange place emotionally, spiritually, and physically. I slept a lot, sometimes 12 hours a night. I continued counseling for the next several years. My body struggled to recover from eight years of trauma and sleep deprivation. Mary Ellen explained that my body didn't believe the trauma had really ended, so it stored up energy by resting.

Through the next year, I discovered cards Sam had written me for my birthday or Mother's Day over the years. "Dear Mommy, thank you for being my mom. I love you, Sam."

But I was not his mother anymore. My heart hurt over that fact.

The hardest question to answer has become: *"How many children do you have?"*

It seems like such an easy question. It gets asked and answered every day in all different settings. It is probably one of the most non-personal questions married women ask each other, but now it felt deeply personal.

The losses. The miscarriage that had taken place. The adoptions that never happened. The babies that could have been. Did any of them count?

I absolutely counted the two children we had raised from birth. But there is another child. This child called me "Mommy" for eight years. He did not die. This child does not live in our home; he does not have our name anymore. But he did. For eight years he was our child.

There was no funeral, no accepted grieving period. There were no condolence cards, no flowers, no church service to mark the passing on of a person from our lives. No public recognition that I had lost a son. No mention of this child again.

For eight years, I held this child, rocked this child, fed this child, clothed this child, housed this child, and schooled this child. I spent hours every week taking this child to specialists, doctors, counselors, therapists, and special education professionals. For four of the eight years, I drove this child weekly to an attachment counselor an hour away. I sat in the waiting room through five surgeries. I took him to 24 rounds of weekly "vision therapy" and put in the hours of required exercises aimed at helping him train his brain to process information better. I drove him to The Children's Hospital for 17 days while he participated in the day psych treatment program.

This was the child chosen for us when we applied to adopt from Vietnam.

The nuns running the orphanage had told us of how they went into their prayer room each time they had a family desiring to adopt. They prayed until they received a unanimous decision regarding which child God had chosen for a family. They believed God had selected Sam to become part of our family.

Adoption is not for the faint of heart. International adoption of an older, special needs child is even more difficult. This child was just three and a half when he became our son. He was almost 12 when he became their son.

How many children do you have?

Do you mean now?

Do you mean how many children have you ever had?

Do you mean how many children have your same name and still call you Mom?

Do you mean how many children do you consider yours in your heart?

Why is this such a difficult question? Depending on the day, or the heart of the person asking, I answer that question differently. Sometimes I answer as you would answer the question, "How are you?" I just say "two." Sometimes I answer "three," and don't explain. Sometimes, when I feel a person is trying to get to know me and they are safe, I tell the truth.

I had three children, but now I have two.

Epilogue

*I*T'S BEEN FIVE years since I've seen my son.

Soon after Sam joined his new family, my marriage went through very turbulent times. It felt as if everything we had to put on the back burner because of Sam's pressing issues came screaming to the surface. We entered marriage counseling, and our whole family struggled with depression.

Family, friends, and our church community just didn't know what to do with us, and we felt horribly isolated.

As time went on, our wounds began to heal, and we began to find a new normal.

Some friends were struggling with their adopted teenage son. He and his mother had the same dynamics as Sam and me. They asked if we would be willing to let their son stay with us on weekends for several months, to give their family a much-needed break. I offered without hesitation. I knew this scenario. I could support, love, and nurture someone else's child with RAD, I just couldn't be the mother to my own. We never had problems when this boy joined us. He cleaned up after himself. He was polite. He was responsible. I knew how his mother felt, and it made me happy to be able to provide the kind of help we so desperately needed for ourselves, but never found.

Our marriage is now back on track, and stronger than ever. Bob and I are working together to create the intimacy we know is available to us. We still struggle sometimes. We've heard that many marriages don't survive the loss of a child. We understand how this happens. The pain is so enormous and raw. Grief seems to swallow up everything good, leaving only hurt in its wake.

We experienced trauma from parenting Sam, and then overwhelming grief in losing our child. When two people grieve differently, and at differing paces, the marriage gets pushed to the breaking point. Ours almost broke. I'm very thankful to God for holding us together, giving hope when things seemed hopeless, and for the many counselors who have loved and guided us through this painful journey.

Not only did Bob and I experience trauma, but Brendan, Katie, and Sam did as well. We are continuing to heal, forgive, and learn to trust each other and other people as well. It's a long process back from trauma. It's not a quick fix, or an easy journey. We've discovered lots of other wounded people along the way. Many of them have chosen to stay stuck, run away from relationships, or now hurt others to try to protect themselves. We learned we can't heal by ourselves, and we didn't have the resources to do this work on our own.

And so it continues.

After prompting from Mary Ellen and Dr. Sanders, I went back to school. In their words, "You've already done all the work, why don't you go get your credentials?" In 2012, I graduated from Liberty University with a degree in Human Services, Marriage and Family Therapy. I knew I didn't want to open a typical counseling practice, because I had so many ideas to go along with helping individuals and couples one-on-one. Later that year, I became a Board Certified Christian Life Coach (BCCLC) through the American Association of Christian Counseling.

Carrie O'Toole Ministries was born in September 2012.

Throughout my schooling, I focused my research on topics relating to attachment and trauma. I discovered that both Bob and I had insecure attachments, which created unhealthy relationship styles and made it very difficult to parent a child with Reactive Attachment Disorder. We have worked to create more secure relationship styles.

Out of my training, I developed a Three-Day Relationship Group Intensive. We meet in the mountains of Colorado to help people understand their own relationship styles and discover how their styles and past traumas impact them. We identify patterns they fall into, and develop tools to help them become more emotionally and relationally secure.

We began "Broken & Brilliant" podcasts in 2014, sharing stories of people who have been through difficult struggles, but somehow found brilliance in the brokenness. We have interviewed million-copy best selling authors, attachment specialists, and professional counselors, and have great plans to reach many people with the message that there is hope beyond the dark times.

We are excited to publish our first films on YouTube in spring 2014. You'll find messages of hope, healing, breath-taking beauty, wisdom, and courage.

Brendan is now 21 years old. He followed his passion by attending film school, and now he works for Carrie O'Toole Ministries. His job includes filming, providing sound, editing, mixing, producing, and publishing my podcasts and films. I truly enjoy the time we get to spend together dreaming up new ideas, filming, and going out to lunch. It's been a time of renewal for us, and I wouldn't trade it for anything.

Katie is 20, and finishing her junior year at the University of Denver. She will earn her Bachelor of Music Performance degree with her French horn, followed by her Master of Education degree. She too pursued her passion, and has become a much better musician than I ever dreamed she'd be. I love listening to her play, and I'm so thankful she attends a school within driving distance, so I can attend all of her concerts. She and I have worked through the hurts of the past and truly enjoy being together. She is one of my favorite girls in the world, and I take every opportunity to spend time shopping, hanging out, and talking with her about her own relationships and attachment style.

We've continued to travel as a family, and find cruising is still our favorite. We feel truly blessed to be able to enjoy this together. I feel God's pleasure in providing this time for our family. I believe he totally under-stands how important it is to have "do-overs" as we each continue to heal, individually and collectively.

Sam continues to struggle with attachment issues, but seems to be doing better with Tom and Kelly. We hear brief updates once in awhile, but don't have regular contact with his new family out of respect for them. We know how draining parenting a child with Sam's past trauma can be, and feel we need to support them from a distance.

As I wrote this book, I realized how traumatic these years were for me. My brain literally couldn't remember many events because the level of grief and depression was so severe. I've learned since that trauma cannot be recalled logically. It's normal to not be able to recall traumatic circumstances. The memories sometimes return as I watch videos, look at photo albums, or talk to friends who knew us during that time.

I've continued to seek answers for dealing with RAD. I believe that one day Sam will again be a part of our lives in some capacity. I want to have resources available to him if he chooses to seek help and healing for his traumatic life. Some of the methods we used are now not considered to be helpful (including holding therapy), but at the time that was the course of treatment recommended. I wish I had known then what I know now. I don't know if it would have changed the outcome for our family, or not.

How to find help for your RAD child:

- Find a therapist who can answer most of your questions without much explanation on your part. If they understand RAD, they will anticipate what you might ask.

- Get help for your own childhood wounds and triggers, so they don't interfere with your attempts to help your child.

- Find an attachment specialist who works with the family. Individual therapy with your child will backfire. It is based on trust, yet your child can't trust. They will manipulate the therapist and act out against mom after therapy.

- It's not helpful to focus on behaviors alone. They are symptoms. Make sure the therapist works to heal the relationship between you and your child. Your children need help giving up control and learning to trust. The behaviors will improve as the relationship heals.

- Out patient therapy works with children exhibiting less severe attachment issues.

- For children with moderate to severe RAD, outpatient treatment doesn't work. The children find ways to redouble their efforts against vulnerability in between sessions.

- In-patient treatment should be done by professional treatment parents trained to stay objective and not get triggered. They are typically parents of RAD children themselves, so they understand, and are prepared for the challenges of healing wounded children. They are compassionate toward the parents struggling so hard to love these children.

- Seek frequent respite. These children often behave worse after the parents return from time away. Make sure respite is frequent enough to make the time worth the pay-back.

My hope is for this book to bring help and healing to many. Even if a child needs to be placed in another home, life is not over. God continues to heal.

Please visit Carrie O'Toole Ministries...

www.carrieotoole.com

Email: carrie@carrieotoole.com

Facebook: Carrie O'Toole Ministries

Twitter: @CarrieO'Toole

YouTube: Carrie O'Toole Ministries.

You'll find video Podcasts featuring attachment experts, authors, counselors, and others sharing stories of moving from Broken to Brilliant. Check out our short films as well.

iTunes: Broken and Brilliant audio podcasts

Made in the USA
San Bernardino, CA
06 May 2014